I0796744

Fascism or Genocide

Fascism or Genocide

How a Decade of Political Disorder Broke American Politics

Ross Barkan

VERSO
London • New York

First published by Verso 2025

Parts of this book originated in reporting or first appeared in the *New York Times Magazine*, *New York* magazine, and *ARC*

The manufacturer's authorized representative in the EU for product safety (GPSR) is LOGOS EUROPE, 9 rue Nicolas Poussin, 17000, La Rochelle, France Contact@logoseurope.eu

1 3 5 7 9 10 8 6 4 2

Verso
UK: 6 Meard Street, London W1F 0EG
US: 207 East 32nd Street, New York, NY 10016
versobooks.com

Verso is the imprint of New Left Books

ISBN-13: 978-1-80429-938-8
ISBN-13: 978-1-80429-940-1 (US EBK)
ISBN-13: 978-1-80428-939-5 (UK EBK)

British Library Cataloguing in Publication Data
A catalogue record for this book is available from the British Library

Library of Congress Cataloging-in-Publication Data
Library of Congress Control Number: 2025934566

Typeset in Sabon LT by Hewer Text UK Ltd, Edinburgh
Printed and bound by CPI Group (UK) Ltd, Croydon CR0 4YY

Contents

1

The Squad

Is this what the counterrevolution looked like?

The congressman, in a bright yellow T-shirt, his muscles tensing in the ludicrous June heat: "We're gonna show fucking AIPAC the motherfucking power of the South Bronx," he said, perhaps echoing ghosts of recent progressive past. *They got money, we got people.*

The people, united, will never be defeated—except they were.

The American Israel Public Affairs Committee, the most powerful pro-Israel organization in America, unleashed nearly $15 million, deluging airwaves and mailboxes to obliterate the congressional career of Jamaal Anthony Bowman, who, in a parallel universe, might have been the first openly socialist senator or governor from New York. In the days before the election, at the start of 2024's chaotic political summer, it was obvious Bowman was going to lose. Obvious to the pundit class, the voters, and even the campaigns themselves. At St. Mary's Park, Bowman had brought all the cavalry—Bernie Sanders, Alexandria Ocasio-Cortez, and Nydia Velázquez, the first Puerto Rican woman elected to Congress—and tried his very best to prop up the crowd, which the campaign claimed numbered about a thousand.

But something was *off*.

Was it the heat? Was it the polls that showed him down the seventeen points he would eventually lose by?

Sanders thundered about the billionaire class trying to buy another election. Ocasio-Cortez, who came on stage dancing to Cardi B, warned that outsiders were "trying to buy our representation because they don't like who we chose to represent us." There were cheers, and signs held aloft; there was genuine enthusiasm mustered in the relentless sun. Some, even, might have remembered being there before, in that very park. They were hoping, Sanders and Ocasio-Cortez in particular, that there were some stray tethers left to that miraculous past, that last day of March, in 2016, when anything seemed possible—when Sanders, a candidate for president of the United States, brought more than 18,000 people to St. Mary's.

That was one subtext of the doomed rally. Ocasio-Cortez, as she reminded the crowd, had been a staffer on that campaign. She was anonymous then, twenty-six, one more infantrywoman in the youth army propelling Sanders into one of the more shocking primaries of modern times. It had all started there, with that first Sanders campaign: the rebirth of the American left, the progressive movement, which had seemed limitless until it hadn't. On March 31, Sanders was in New York to contest the primary against Hillary Clinton, who not that long ago had been the state's junior senator. Clinton was ahead—she was always ahead—but Sanders would just not *go away*. He had nearly won Iowa. He won New Hampshire outright. Defying public polling, he had beaten her back in Michigan, and his volunteer army only swelled larger and larger. Here he came, the cantankerous left-wing sage from the wilds of Vermont, such an outsider that he refused to identify as a Democrat, winning millions of votes and the delegates that came with them.

Here he was, to Clinton's great disdain, believing he could win in New York State.

Everywhere Sanders went, crowds. Delirious thousands, most of them too young to remember the Cold War, cheering on the man who called himself a socialist and promised it all—free healthcare, free college tuition, an end to the nightmare of income inequality. What separated Sanders from the socialists of old was his understanding of the American political system. The two-party duopoly had savagely thwarted his idol, Eugene Debs, and eventually eradicated a Socialist Party that once boasted more than a thousand office holders across America and at least two members of Congress. Sanders was not a member of the Democratic Socialists of America (DSA), but he implicitly operated in the shadow of Michael Harrington, the renowned author and activist who was the group's founder. Harrington's insight was startlingly simple: Leftists will only win in America by competing in Democratic primaries. They cannot be third-party rogues, Socialists or Greens, and hope to ever wield power. Sanders never became a Democrat, but he caucused with the Democrats in the Senate. He voted like them. And when he ran for president, he was, even if technically an independent, one of them.

He would take more than 1,800 delegates to the Democratic convention that summer in Philadelphia.

The St. Mary's rally, on the last day of March, came several weeks before the primary. Sanders was a remarkable draw; for those who flowed into the park in the working-class, heavily Latino neighborhood of the Bronx, he was something of a revelation. Thousands jammed a baseball field on the other end of the park just to watch him on a big screen, while thick lines snaked around the block to mass through security. He spoke from a stage on a blacktop with public housing towers at his back as his fans chanted, waved signs, and cheered the political revolution they viewed as inevitable. Rosario Dawson and Spike Lee were his surrogates that night. The famed director insisted older voters backing Clinton had to "get their minds right." "The old generation, they're on this Clinton thing," he sneered.

Virtually every politician, labor union, and political club endorsed Clinton in the primary. She had the support of Andrew Cuomo, the strongman governor, and both of the state's senators, Kirsten Gillibrand and Chuck Schumer, the future Senate majority leader. She had the firm backing of the state's House delegation, the local legislators, city council members, and even the mayor of New York City, Bill de Blasio, who was a professed Sanders admirer. Political machines, as Ocasio-Cortez would prove within a couple years, were emaciated, but there was plenty of money and power in politics and it was all marshaled behind Clinton. In New York, there was perhaps no greater example of insurgent versus establishment, outsider versus insider. Sanders had grown up in a rent-controlled Brooklyn apartment; as far as the state's political operators were concerned, he was a persona non grata—a pest.

And Sanders didn't have much regard for them either. "You could say moving to Vermont was the best decision I ever made," he told a journalist in 2014. "What would have happened if I'd stayed in Brooklyn? How far could I have gotten? The State Assembly?"

New York offered no miracles for Sanders, but he managed a respectable 42 percent of the statewide vote, enough to hand him a sizable delegate haul and the unstinting admiration of the twenty-somethings who had lived their best political lives through his campaign. Ocasio-Cortez, of course, was one of them. Another was a woman named Julia Salazar, who would become DSA's first member of the New York State Senate when AOC joined Congress. DSA, hypercharged by Sanders and catalyzed further by Donald Trump's victory—terror, disgust, and rage are tools for organizing, too—exploded, evolving rapidly from a glorified discussion group for tetchy college professors and inveterate *Dissent* subscribers to the premier hub for any kind of politicking a left-wing American under thirty might attempt.

For so long an *ideas* organization, DSA now had literal foot soldiers. They passed out leaflets, knocked on doors, raised money, and packed out meetings. Clinton's loss to Trump knocked her off the political chessboard, but Sanders was still a sitting senator. There was another campaign to look forward to, another chance to right the wrongs of 2016. And DSA was not alone. A loose constellation of progressive organizations, all skeptical of capitalism if not explicitly socialistic like DSA, took shape. They included Justice Democrats, which helped recruit Ocasio-Cortez to run for Congress and quickly gained influence among leftists. The Working Families Party (WFP)—a hybrid of labor unions and activist organizations that first took root in New York State in the 1990s and eventually formed a national arm—had endorsed Ocasio-Cortez's opponent, Joe Crowley, in that famed 2018 congressional race. But once AOC triumphed, the WFP quickly aligned itself with her and with the group of congressional Democrats, including Bowman, who would join the left-wing House faction known as the Squad. They would atone for missing so badly in that Crowley primary.

DSA, WFP, Justice Democrats—all made Bowman their cause célèbre in 2024. He had first won at the beginning of the pandemic summer of 2020, ousting Eliot Engel, a longtime Bronx and Westchester congressman who chaired the foreign affairs committee. Engel was a conventional Democrat, with foreign policy views that skewed hawkish: He had voted for the Iraq War and the Patriot Act, and was an enthusiastic, unyielding supporter of Israel, even as the government veered rightward. When Bowman ran against Engel, foreign policy was not overly relevant, though the insurgent didn't waste time touting his own leftist views and making "jobs and education, not bombs and incarceration" a calling card of his campaign.

If Crowley, an aging Irish American political boss, was the ultimate foil for Ocasio-Cortez, a twenty-eight-year-old Puerto Rican who had never run for office before, Engel wasn't much different for Bowman. One was a white septuagenarian ladder climber who had fought in the trenches of local Democratic politics since the 1970s. The other was a Black former middle school principal and proud hip-hop head who celebrated, on his school's "Wall of Honor," the Black militants and Assata Shakur, a convicted murderer who fled to Cuba, as well as Mutulu Shakur, who served a lengthy prison sentence for armed robbery, along with the likes of more mainstream figures including Barack Obama, Sonia Sotomayor, and Langston Hughes.

Both Ocasio-Cortez and Bowman had excellent timing. The young AOC, a former Sanders organizer, was embarking on a campaign during what would be an apex for left political organizing in America—the midterm of Donald Trump's first presidency. While ideological fracture had defined the 2016 political season, with Sanders and Clinton supporters bitterly warring through the convention and beyond, Trump's black swan victory had united, temporarily, all factions of the Democratic Party against him. Moderates, liberals, progressives, and socialists all reviled Trump. And they were motivated, like never before in the young century, to *practice* politics. Crowley's Queens Democratic Party, as well as other local political organizations, thrived on indifference. The Queens machine, as it was called, was hardly a political machine anymore—the clubs were not teeming with volunteers, there was no finely tuned door-to-door turnout operation, and it could not reasonably whip thousands of voters toward a given candidate. Its primary domains, in the 2010s, were the exceedingly low turnout judicial elections and control of the local surrogate's court, where the estates of those who died without wills were processed and lawyers close to Crowley reaped millions. Crowley and his candidates for various local offices—the city council, the state assembly, the state senate—won because they either ran unopposed or faced little in the way of serious competition.

Local politics, in AOC and Bowman's New York, had grown static. Starting in 2017, Trump's first year in office, that all began to change. Activists, many of them young and college educated, began paying attention to the elections in their backyard. They formed their own organizations independent of the political clubs. Many focused chiefly on driving Republicans out of office or electing Democrats who were less conservative—especially those willing to challenge a caucus of Democrats in the New York State legislature that had formed a power-sharing agreement with the Republicans, who still sat in the majority. Ocasio-Cortez's victory in June 2018 would help power the insurgent progressive Democrats running in the state primaries that September; having become, upon defeating Crowley, an instant national sensation, she lent her newfound fame and fundraising prowess to the cause of local Democratic politics.

Both Ocasio-Cortez and Bowman were willing to identify as democratic socialists and work with DSA. To men like Crowley and Engel, who came of age during the Cold War, this was unfathomable. They had both spent their careers in the absolute mainstream of Democratic politics, and seemed most comfortable when the party, under Bill Clinton, embraced supply-side economics, globalization, and a shrinking of the social safety net. The new DSA activists loathed neoliberalism; if they could not always agree on what socialism in the United States should actually look like, they knew what they did not want: unfettered markets, deregulation, privatization, and American military intervention in foreign conflicts.

It would be a mistake, though, to suggest that the AOC and Bowman triumphs, of 2018 and 2020, respectively, were evidence of one ideology crushing another in the electoral arena. American politics is never so straightforward. If the two Democrats plainly ran to the left of the powerful incumbents, they both had one other potent arrow in their quivers: They could claim they were fully rooted in the districts where they ran. *Authenticity* is a tired political term, but in the twenty-first century it's retained a great deal of relevance among Democratic and Republican politicians alike. In a hyper-real world mediated by social media and digital fakery, voters hunger for politicians who seem *real* to them—and one sign of reality is rootedness. Are you from here? Or, absent that, have you adopted the customs of the place? Do you *seem* like you belong?

Ocasio-Cortez was not eager to share with voters and the media that she spent her formative years in Yorktown Heights, a middle-class town in the New York suburb of Westchester County. Rather, her campaign would be about the Bronx—working class to poor, and heavily Spanish-speaking—and how she was born there and still lived there, strategically eliding that she had grown up in Yorktown and graduated from its public high school. Crowley was a product of the Queens portion of the district but had moved his family to a Virginia suburb close to Washington, DC, where he spent most of his time methodically climbing the ranks of Congress. This was an arrangement that was not uncommon in the twentieth century; another powerful New York congressman, Steve Solarz, kept a sprawling house in the tony Virginia suburb of McClean, and maintained, as his address in Brooklyn, his mother-in-law's home. Crowley was quieter than Solarz—who enjoyed entertaining dignitaries in Virginia—because customs had changed. It took a 2011 *New York Post* exposé to bring Crowley's Virginia residence to public attention—he was sending his children to the Arlington public schools and living in a house that, in 2004, had been purchased for nearly $700,000. But even then, no candidates emerged to challenge him. Ocasio-Cortez wouldn't announce her bid until 2017. "A lot of progressive groups are coming out of the woodwork. They've been trying to find a challenger to Crowley for years," Ocasio-Cortez told me at the time. "It's literally political suicide for anyone with a semblance of a political career."

One of the more stirring political ads of the twenty-first century would come from that first Ocasio-Cortez campaign. It was a work of messaging genius, engineered for virality. Two minutes in length, the ad was produced for YouTube, and intended to introduce AOC to the wider electorate as she gained visible momentum against Crowley. "This race is about people versus money," Ocasio-Cortez said, performing her own voiceover. "It's time we acknowledge that not all Democrats are the same—that a Democrat who takes corporate money, profits off foreclosure, doesn't live here, doesn't send his kids to our schools, doesn't drink our water or breathe our air cannot possibly represent us."

Bowman's pitch, two years later, would end up mirroring AOC's. When he announced his campaign, it wasn't widely known that Engel, who had been a member of

Congress since 1989, owned a home in Maryland. And if it weren't for the Covid-19 pandemic, his residence may have gone unreported or little noticed. In March 2020, three months before the June primary, coronavirus ravaged New York City. Residents with the means or the ability fled; one of them was Congressman Engel. In May, an *Atlantic* reporter found him living in his suburban Maryland home. "I'm in both places," Engel insisted. His fate would be sealed in June when he was heard disparaging an in-district press conference he was attending. "If I didn't have a primary, I wouldn't care," he told another Bronx Democratic politician.

Bowman easily vanquished Engel. As a candidate who emphasized social justice causes and openly backed defunding the police, Bowman found himself, like AOC, in an ideal political moment. It was the summer of 2020. Police had killed George Floyd at the end of May, and the Black Lives Matter movement, quasi-moribund after the rapid rise it had enjoyed in the middle of the 2010s, was resurgent and radicalized. The 2014 and 2015 marches had called for reforming police departments. Now, in 2020, it was suddenly de rigueur to call for the gutting of them, or the total abolition of police. Progressive and openly socialist Democrats like Bowman were not unconflicted on this front—it was a question of whether, in the wake of Floyd's death, police departments should still exist. Few, if any, politicians wanted total abolition, but even mainstream Democrats who had voted, only a few years earlier, to hire more police in New York in a bid to reform the department were now enthusiastically demanding budget cuts. For some, policing itself was an original American evil, a sin that supposedly dated back to the slave patrols of the nineteenth century. Getting police out of the way would only help.

Police reform had not been at the center of Ocasio-Cortez's 2018 campaign because Black Lives Matter, by then, had receded. Thanks to Trump's aggressive policing of the border, abolishing ICE—Immigration and Customs Enforcement—was the most popular progressive demand. Ocasio-Cortez had not been involved with DSA before her campaign but, after taking their endorsement, she mostly embraced their immigration policies: the majority of young socialists supported open borders. Here, they diverged from both the American working class—unchecked immigration was not popular—and Sanders himself, who had derided the concept of mass migration to the United States. He called open borders a "Koch brothers proposal" (in reference to the right-wing, libertarian billionaires who had lavishly funded Republican causes) and argued that while "we've got to work with the rest of the industrialized world to address the problems of international poverty," this wasn't done by "making people in this country even poorer."

Sanders may have been the patron saint of the young, surging, and unabashedly progressive left, but he would not give ground on some of their most cherished causes; as a consequence, by the end of his second presidential campaign, he began to lose influence with them. He did not want to end border enforcement nor, to the chagrin of DSA and other activist organizations, did he want to defund police departments. "Do I think we should not have police departments in America?" Sanders said in June 2020, less than two weeks after Floyd was killed. "No, I don't. There's no city in the world that does not have police departments." He called, instead, for departments to have "well-educated, well-trained, well-paid professionals." Activists despaired. AOC and Bowman still supported Sanders, but it was apparent *his* particular concerns—single-payer healthcare, raising taxes on the wealthy—were no longer overriding enchantments for the young who wanted to protest and protest again. Stopping the police and combating racism—along with, finally, getting fresh air in that hothouse pandemic summer—would matter most to those fueling the largest protest marches since the 1960s.

American politics and culture are more cyclical than most in the trenches would readily admit. Issues that once felt so urgent that they were worth crafting sole identities around can suddenly matter much less—and this seemed truer than ever as the fast twitch 2010s gave way to the 2020s. As that decade reached its midpoint, insurgents didn't have to be progressive any longer. This was Bowman's plight in the spring of 2024. He was not Engel—he had served in Congress less than four years and very much resided in the district, full-time—but he had, in his rise to political celebrity, made himself vulnerable to some of the same attacks he had leveled against the elderly congressman during the pandemic.

George Latimer, a veteran Democratic politician, was uniquely situated to snuff out the political career of one of the progressive left's brightest stars. In the 16th Congressional District, which roped in much of his Westchester turf and a sliver of the northern Bronx, Latimer was as strong a challenger as one could fathom. He had been the Westchester County executive since 2017, and before that a state legislator and county elected official. Unlike Engel, he was ubiquitous, known for his willingness to show up at every ribbon cutting, parade, little league opening day, and chicken dinner. He was a hyperlocal analogue of Chuck Schumer, New York's senior senator and the Democratic majority leader, a hustling *macher* celebrated (and occasionally derided) for his endless string of public appearances. Latimer was inarguably *of* the district—he passed the authenticity test, and voters were not going to treat him like a typical insurgent. If anything, he was arguably more of a household name within Westchester than Bowman.

But why was Latimer, at age seventy, trying to depose his own congressman?

When I met Bowman that April, at a Mexican restaurant in the heavily Latino village of Port Chester, he was tired of talking about Latimer's decision to run against him. "Yeah, I mean, I think it says something about his character, his integrity, and his actual leadership for the district. But enough of him. When are we going to talk about *me*?"

Munching on chicken empanadas, Bowman was in a cheery mood, despite my prodding on Latimer. The night before, Summer Lee, a fellow progressive in Congress, had survived a furious primary challenge, and Bowman sensed a pattern. "Salut!" he called out. "I'm excited, hopefully, for the whole progressive movement to zero in on NY-16. Let's get to work."

The movement did show up for Bowman. Justice Democrats, the Working Families Party, DSA, and a few major labor unions, including 1199 SEIU, the healthcare workers' union which remains the largest in New York, endorsed him. Still, he was endangered, and getting vastly outraised—and outspent—by Latimer, thanks to the American Israel Public Affairs Committee. "They do not want any critique, they do not want any accountability, and so what it looks like to people in my district and around the country is that Israel can do whatever it wants even though, to people on the outside looking in, it looks completely wrong and horrible," Bowman told me. "One, it doesn't represent all the Jews. It doesn't represent all the Jews in Israel!"

"If Israel represents all the Jews," Bowman continued, revving up now, "and if Israel is doing bad things without accountability, some idiot in the street just makes the connection that, *Oh, Jews must be bad because Israel is bad*. That's fucking—excuse my language—that's effing scary, man, and dangerous. And as we fight antisemitism, that has to include accountability for Israel."

There was a time, not very long ago, when no member of Congress would dare speak that way. The slaughter of October 7, though, had catalyzed a new era, as Israel suffered a mass casualty terrorist attack and retaliated by shelling Gaza and killing tens of thousands of Palestinians. Protesters flooded the streets and rocked college campuses, including two, Columbia and City College, that were only a short drive from Westchester. Bowman had become an AIPAC target for his support of conditioning military aid to Israel and his willingness to label the IDF campaign in Gaza a "genocide," among other criticisms lodged at the Jewish state. "AIPAC is one of the most powerful lobbies in America. Well you know what we have got to say to AIPAC? Bring it on," Bowman said at his campaign kickoff. "AIPAC, bring it on. We are not scared of none of that. I'm from the streets of New York."

The streets of New York, ideologically and culturally, remained fraught. I met Latimer at the Mount Vernon Metro North station, where he was dutifully passing out palm cards ("Good morning, I'm George Latimer, I'm on the ballot") to the few dreary commuters who ambled through. A couple lit up when they recognized him, and one man, who was white, seemed to lament "identity politics" while promising his vote to Latimer. As much as it had become about Israel, it was easy to make the primary about *race*: Latimer was the white ethnic, Irish and Italian, trying to dethrone a congressman who had told me racism was the number-one issue facing the district and that he viewed himself, as the first Black man to hold this congressional seat, as a role model to Black youth throughout the area.

Latimer was the ideal AIPAC recruit. He admitted to me that they had asked him to run, though he deemed himself a "reluctant bride." Funded by right-wing, Republican donors, AIPAC traditionally doled out large contributions to powerful Democratic and Republican politicians alike in a bid to forge an unbreakable pro-Israel consensus on Capitol Hill. What changed, in the early 2020s, was AIPAC's decision—along with another aligned political action committee known as Democratic Majority for Israel (DMFI)—to intervene in Democratic congressional primaries. AIPAC established a new super PAC, the anodyne-sounding United Democracy Project, to unleash millions against left-leaning Democrats who were not, in their view, properly supporting the revanchist Netanyahu government. Together, AIPAC and DMFI had successfully bludgeoned several progressive Democrats, including Nina Turner, a close Bernie Sanders ally who tried to win an Ohio House seat, and Andy Levin, a Jewish congressman from Michigan who was the nephew of Carl Levin—a longtime Michigan senator—and the son of Sander Levin, a veteran congressman from the state.

Before his election to Congress in 2018, Andy Levin had been the president of his synagogue. In Washington, he hoped to work toward the establishment of a Palestinian state that would also guarantee Israel as a Jewish haven. Levin labored for several years on the Two-State Solution Act, which would have recognized the West Bank, East Jerusalem, and Gaza as occupied territories inconsistent with international law (a designation rejected at the time by the Secretary of State, Mike Pompeo) and curtailed settlement expansion. He also supported conditioning military aid to Israel.

Liberal organizations applauded him. His fellow Democrats were more wary. One, who was a co-sponsor of the Act, backed away once a competitive election loomed. "He came up to me on the floor," Levin told me, "and he said to me, 'Andy, I have to get off the bill.' He was very clear about it. It was just because of AIPAC, and he couldn't deal with that."

In 2022, the state's new congressional district map meant that Levin found himself competing with a Democratic colleague, Haley Stevens, for a seat. AIPAC spent more than $4 million to boost Stevens, an avowed Israel hawk. Levin's congressional career was over.

"My colleagues certainly took a lesson like: 'Well, gosh, Andy Levin was such a pure soul. Too bad he got wiped out by AIPAC,' " he said. "It was not a subtle message."

Conservative forces could decide, Levin feared, to pump enormous amounts of cash into primaries, distorting Democratic platforms. "When you think about it, there's no difference between the right-wing-on-Israel group and any other group that is anathema to progressive politics coming in and saying, 'Well, in each Democratic primary, we'll pick the candidate more to our liking.' " Without discussing Bowman directly—I had spoken with the ex-congressman when Latimer's candidacy was still nascent—Levin had offered a roadmap of what was to come. AIPAC, along with DMFI, were going to break every spending record to ensure Bowman didn't get another term in Congress.

The expenditures were astronomical. Latimer, never a prolific fundraiser before, quickly banked more than $3 million for himself at the close of March—double Bowman's haul—and had top donors who were either AIPAC-affiliated or cut checks to Donald Trump, including Alex Campos, Alex Dubitsky, and Stephen and Carolyn Lauro, who once hosted a Long Island fundraiser for Trump. Latimer insisted to me none of this cash would influence his political views. "I'm not even soliciting them. I have an event, they send checks. It's not going to change what I do in Congress," he said that spring. This was difficult to believe, given how staunchly supportive of Israel and the Netanyahu government Latimer had become. He refused to offer any criticism of the Israeli military's conduct in Gaza, and would not endorse Chuck Schumer's view that Benjamin Netanyahu shouldn't be prime minister any longer. He also rejected any calls for a ceasefire in the war.

On the AIPAC cash spent in his favor, he merely said that Bowman had provoked them by not being as fierce an ally as he. "If Mike Tyson was in the room and I decided to go over to Mike Tyson and say, 'Hey Mike Tyson, bring it on, yo,' what do I think Mike Tyson might do to me? Whatever I used to be, I wouldn't be the same person after he finished with me."

Meanwhile, the progressive left learned another difficult lesson during the most expensive House primary in American history: money always goes further when there's campaign fodder at the outset. If AOC and Bowman rose to power in a similar fashion, as thrilling and charismatic outsiders, it was Bowman who could not keep himself from being embroiled in controversy. Ocasio-Cortez, for all her time in the spotlight and the ways in which she welcomed her role as a right-wing hate object, had evolved into a disciplined political actor; it helped, too, that her journey into electoral politics had not been so curious. As Bowman campaigned against Latimer, reports surfaced of old blog posts he had written that appeared to lend credence to 9/11 conspiracy theories. His YouTube page was also following alienating conspiracy accounts. And he faced a House censure for pulling a false fire alarm when Democrats were trying to stall a vote, which Bowman told me was an accident and Latimer believed was intentional.

All of this contributed to an image the progressive left had been trying to counteract since their politicians found success in the wake of the first Sanders campaign—the idea that they were too radical and ultimately unserious about governing. Bowman was the congressman who pulled the fire alarm. Latimer would be the congressman who didn't. Throughout the primary, Latimer lashed Bowman for this while cementing his local ties; he racked up far more endorsements from town elected officials and Democratic organizations. Whatever was left of the Westchester machine went for Latimer. Bowman's national profile wasn't playing well back home. "He has a different brand of politics which appeals more so to getting clicks and likes and retweets and making headlines versus someone who has delivered," Tyrae Woodson-Samuels, the majority leader of the Westchester County Board of Legislators and a Latimer supporter, argued to me before the election.

One peculiar dynamic of the primary that was never examined closely enough was how the two Democrats polarized in opposite directions. Latimer grew more conservative as Bowman veered left. Before the two men had run against each other, Latimer was a center-left Democrat in good standing with local progressive organizations and even the Working Families Party, which had handed him their ballot line in previous elections. Bowman was an unabashed leftist and withering critic of capitalism who nevertheless was inching nearer to the center; he broke with DSA in 2021 after a select number of chapters attempted to expel him over his vote to fund the Iron Dome missile defense system in Israel. Socialist activists derided him for taking a trip to

Israel sponsored by J Street, a liberal Zionist organization that was trying to become the left's counter to AIPAC. Anti-Zionists disliked J Street because it did not support a single, binational state for Israelis and Palestinians and it strongly opposed the Boycotts, Divestments, and Sanctions (BDS) movement, which sought to isolate Israel internationally by promoting nonviolent cultural boycotts of the government. For socialists and pro-Palestinian leftists, Bowman had become something of a quisling, too willing to appease establishment Democrats.

This changed once AIPAC declared open war on Bowman. He began calling Israel's killing of Palestinian civilians a "genocide" and lost J Street's endorsement. He heaped praise on the cerebral and stridently anti-Israel scholar Norman Finkelstein, who initially described the Hamas attacks of October 7 as a "heroic resistance" akin to the Warsaw Ghetto uprising, writing that it "warms every fiber of my soul." Ocasio-Cortez, and certainly Sanders, would have recognized the risk of appearing with Finkelstein—Bowman had introduced him at a panel discussion in Westchester—in a congressional district with a large Jewish and Israel-supporting population. Bowman won, again, the support of DSA, promising to openly back the BDS movement, something he had never done as a congressman. And, in his conversations with me, he seemed to embrace the one-state solution for Israel and the Palestinians that was vehemently opposed by almost every American politician in both parties.

I asked Bowman directly if Israel should always have a Jewish majority. He didn't answer in the affirmative. "It might have been the day after or definitely the weekend after we won against Congressman Engel—who's my guy, Peter Beinart, wrote a one-state piece that I thought was brilliant, I thought it was phenomenal," he said. "Some of this stuff is, like, I'm not Jewish, man, you know? So I don't want to be talking out of turn about Jewish issues. I'm also not Palestinian, right? It's the same kind of deal but because my values are rooted in human rights and I know my district well, I have to comment on these things. And I do."

"I want Palestinians to be free from occupation and apartheid and I want Jews to be safe—and Palestinians to be safe, of course. How do we do that?" he added. "Jews should have a safe place to exist. What that looks like, the details of that, let's figure that out. That is not Jews are safe, Palestinians are under occupation—those two things can't co-exist anymore."

It is plausible Bowman will be on the right side of history in the sense of where the Democratic Party, on Israel, could end up. Joe Biden could be the last Democratic president to be resolutely and unflinchingly pro-Israel; voters under thirty-five take a dim view of an ethno-nationalist nation racing rightward, and these views, with time, are bound to calcify. Generational shifts are real. Biden, born before the establishment of Israel, came of age when Zionism and liberalism were intertwined, when young men like Bernard Sanders of

Brooklyn could travel to a kibbutz in the hopes of finding socialism in the desert. Israel's triumph in the Six-Day War made Zionism, for a number of years, seem all-American, the blood-streaked survivors of the Holocaust winning, somehow, their own version of the Revolutionary War. Supporting Israel was bipartisan, and tolerance for dissent waned in both political parties as the twentieth century drew to a close. In the early 1990s, it was still possible for a Republican president, George H. W. Bush, to withhold loan guarantees to Israel until he was satisfied that the money borrowed with American assistance would not go toward Israeli settlements in the Palestinian territories. Bush, speaking with the American media, even portrayed himself as an underdog battling the might of AIPAC: "I heard today there was something like 1,000 lobbyists on the Hill working on the other side of the question. We've got one lonely little guy down here doing it," he told White House reporters. No president since then has replicated Bush's willingness to so forcefully confront the Israeli government.

On the Democratic side that will change because neither young liberals nor working-class Black and Latino voters are especially enamored with Israel. Those most ardently supportive of Israel are voting Republican: evangelical Christians and Orthodox Jews. Polarization will, with time, come for the issue of Israel in the United States, with a Republican Party in lockstep with an Israeli government that shares its ideology and a

Democratic Party that largely agrees on imposing conditions, like Bush once did, on military aid. Mainstream Democrats will not, in any foreseeable future, be anti-Zionist or entertain the concept of an Israel that is not explicitly Jewish in population and character, even as democracy can only for so long be compatible with an enforced ethno-nationalism. What Democrats will do is migrate, slowly, in Bowman's direction—even if he's not in elected office to reap the political fruits of this transition.

Bowman won a decisive fourteen-point victory over Engel in 2020. Latimer defeated Bowman by an even wider margin in 2024, besting him by seventeen points. It was end of what can be deemed the Progressive Primary Era, which began, in earnest, with the statewide victories Sanders racked up against Clinton in 2016, when he was able to enter the Democratic convention with the largest delegate haul of any insurgent in decades. It continued with the rise of Ocasio-Cortez, the growth of her Squad, and the expansion of DSA. To wage a primary in the 2010s was to confront a self-satisfied establishment that never took the idea of political competition all that seriously. Crowley never fathomed he could actually lose to Ocasio-Cortez, and Engel didn't think he'd suffer any harm at the ballot box if he scurried down to Maryland for a few months during the worst pandemic in a century. Future incumbents—as well as institutional players like Latimer—would not make the same mistakes. Latimer campaigned like he was behind, treating Bowman as a threat. And thanks to his strident, even reactionary, defense of Israel's conduct in Gaza, he was a financial juggernaut.

How were the progressive left to reckon with this—with Bowman's fall in June 2024, and the AIPAC-funded defeat of another Squad congress member, Cori Bush of Missouri, that August? In truth, events had rushed along so quickly, so deliriously, that it seemed whenever a moment of panic or even reckoning might come, that *indigenous American berserk*—to quote Philip Roth—would prevent it. This was the reality of Bernie Sanders's defeat in 2020, when the pandemic obscured what was a devastating loss for his campaign in Michigan, where his working-class movement was supposed to flourish. Bowman lost two days before the eighty-one-year-old Biden debated Trump for the first time in the 2024 presidential race. Biden's failure became the dominant media narrative. Ocasio-Cortez herself, who had stumped so forcefully for the doomed Bowman, was drafted into a new cause, one that would've been startling to any of the foot soldiers of the 2020 campaign: a full-throated, unambiguous defense of Biden, even as a growing chorus of Democrats were demanding he drop out. The leftist outsider who had dethroned a possible future speaker, and later occupied Nancy Pelosi's office to bring attention to climate change, was now arguing that Biden, the man who had crushed Sanders and ended any imminent hopes of an openly socialist American president, should remain on the ticket. "The matter is closed," Ocasio-Cortez insisted. "Joe Biden is our nominee. He is not leaving this race. He is in this race, and I support him."

Of course, AOC was wrong.

Her statement was a recognition of what Biden, domestically at least, *had* done for the left. With a 50–50 Senate majority and Sanders chairing the budget committee, the Biden administration engineered sweeping legislation to fund new infrastructure investments, green energy, and to combat climate change, along with trying to revive the American industrial base by kickstarting the manufacturing of crucial semiconductor chips. With the assistance of Sanders and Democrats in the Senate, Biden was able to force Medicare to negotiate the cost of prescription drugs and cap the price of insulin. His chair of the Federal Trade Commission, Lina Khan, had returned anti-trust enforcement to the American scene. Just as important, progressives felt that they had a direct line to the Biden administration—that sympathetic aides like Ron Klain, Biden's first chief of staff, would listen to them far more than any other elite Democrats had. And this was mostly true. Klain was certainly an enormous departure from the men who had wielded power in the Obama administration, including Rahm Emanuel, the perennial left-loather.

If, by the summer of 2024, Bowman was finished and Biden was reeling, progressives could at least look to what they had salvaged. AOC was on a glide path back to Congress. Sanders, at eighty-two, was running for another term in the Senate. Unlike Biden, he was still capable of delivering rousing speeches and debating opponents. Had he somehow won in 2020, he would have been positioned, at the very minimum, to make a vigorous case for himself in 2024.

Looming over it all was Donald Trump, who, on July 13 of that year, was nearly murdered.

2

Trump

Donald Trump's would-be assassin, Thomas Matthew Crooks, died at twenty. Born two years after the destruction of the Twin Towers, Crooks was eleven when Trump descended the golden escalator. This meant, for nearly half his life, he was subsumed into the life and myth of Donald J. Trump, American President, that his waking moments of intellectual maturity—in those alien years before he tried, very desperately, to insert himself into history—were hardened, bent, and fired by a political leviathan unlike any other who had trundled across our land. Trump, like Andy Warhol, Elvis Presley, and even Lee Harvey Oswald, was indisputably American. Trump was our inheritance, and he was what this titanic empire, as glorious as it was savage, had naturally disgorged. Trump was America's demented world spirit. Of course he would, though bloodied, pump his fist.

Trump was a criminal, a pathological liar, a narcissist, and an inveterate bully. He had few deeply held beliefs. As a politician, he had no regard for the mechanics of government or the analysis of policy. He was, as his critics charged, vacant. And he was also a *genius*—not in the sense of having a soaring IQ or an aptitude for the sciences or an ability to make computations that most human brains cannot. He was, in no way, an intellectual. His genius was all-American, wholly *for publicity*, for having the native foresight, buried deep in his viscous core, to understand what he had to do. He had to perform. He had to shout *fight*, he had to hunt out the cameras, he had to get his fist in the air, he had to apprehend, somehow, what this all meant before the secret service barreled him away. He himself, in the hospital, seemed astounded by his own power. "A lot of people say it's the most iconic photo they've ever seen," he told Michael Goodwin, the sycophantic *New York Post* columnist. "They're right and I didn't die. Usually you have to die to have an iconic picture." This was the platonic ideal of a Trump quote: self-aggrandizing, incorrect, and aimed straight, like an arrow into the heart, at all he would ever care about and all he had gained. He was known. He was forever known. He had fame, and the best kind, the American kind, that which, like Cronos, devoured whatever else was on this Earth, so men and women in Paris and Egypt and Kampala could think of him and dream of him and even bear his likeness, *this* image of the blood and the flag and the fist, on a cotton T-shirt. What else, near death, could Trump long for? The presidency was beside the point. Trump had no genius for governing or genuinely dominating others; he could not, like Napoleon, stand up a new empire or, like the Nazis, make fascism as real as the gun pressed to your temple. His political machine ran on the exhaust fumes of his own mania, and it could do little to discipline the states, the little republics of federalism that would choose, if governed by Democrats, to shirk Trumpism.

Those who try to kill tend to be young and tend to be male. It was mostly forgotten that Oswald, with his wife and receding hairline, was just twenty-four when he took aim at John F. Kennedy from the Texas School Book Depository. In youth, there is a particular ambition that can meld with madness and irrepressible rage. Everything is possible and nothing is possible. Motives are rarely narratives, like we so long for—even if Crooks had left behind a manifesto, which he did not, the true motivations of an attempted murder of the kind inextricably bound to spectacle will always be, to some degree, muddled. One would-be assassin tried to kill a president to impress Jodie Foster. Another, the rare female shooter, wanted to spark a vague, violent revolution to overthrow the powers-that-be. William McKinley was killed by a lonely, unemployed anarchist. The man who killed James Garfield believed, very wrongly, he had been passed over for administration jobs he deserved. The assassination attempt on Trump, then, was something of a throwback. For reasons that few have properly explicated, shooters had lost interest in world leaders. In the twenty-first century, young, gun-obsessed men like Crooks headed for schools, shopping malls, movie theaters, and nightclubs, where the victims were anonymous and defenseless. If Crooks craved fame on the scale of what Trump enjoyed, he failed dramatically. A missed shot is a historical footnote, a Wikipedia page visited less and less with each passing year. It is a curiosity, one more hunk of data to be recalled about the 2020s and the second (albeit short-lived) collision between Donald Trump and Joe Biden, two elderly presidents who had, in divergent fashions, effectively held their political parties hostage, producing a showdown that revolted millions of Americans.

Regardless, the left, and the Democrats broadly, lacked anyone with Trump's genius for seizing attention and never letting it go.

That was obvious at the 2024 Republican National Convention in Milwaukee, which effectively served to sanctify Trump. He sat all week in his box at the convention with a detached, almost beatific smile on his face. This might have been because many of the speakers said he was blessed by God, that it was divine intervention which had ensured the would-be assassin's bullet missed. He might have looked this way because one of his handpicked federal judges, Aileen Cannon, had dealt a possible deathblow to the classified documents indictment, the one that would, if it ever saw a trial, probably stick. He could have been exulting in his ludicrously good fortune. Bankruptcies, sex scandals, a felony conviction, civil judgments, and an ear-flaying bullet had not stopped him. Here he was, at seventy-eight, the Republican nominee for president for the third consecutive time. It was hard to imagine any politician having been loved as fervently as Trump has been by those who support him. The convention in Milwaukee was the real, live sanctification of a human being.

A delegate led the convention in applause while wearing an enormous cardboard Trump mask. Others donned baseball jerseys with "Trump 24" on the back. A man in full Uncle Sam regalia sang about stolen elections to the tune of "All About That Bass," as Peter Navarro, freshly sprung from prison, waved to his adoring fans at the Hyatt Regency, where the military stood guard. Merch was for sale everywhere. Biden's face, superimposed on the Chef Boyardee logo, could have ended up a favorite, if not for the twist coming in just a few days. It read *Chef Boy Are We Fucked.*

One thought kept going through my brain the week of the Republican convention: the delegates were incredibly confident Trump was going to win in November. Everyone there was giddy for the future, like fans of a team that just ran away with the division and was now ready for the first playoff game.

Of course they had reason to be. Polls showed Trump with a durable and burgeoning lead, as Biden's disastrous debate performance on June 27, 2024, further eroded his support in battleground states. Life, certainly, was miserable for Democrats. Democratic elites, who had spent two years pretending Biden's advanced age wasn't a problem, now wanted to dump him but didn't quite know how. They were figuring it out.

All of it felt a lot like 2016, only in reverse. When I covered the 2016 Democratic convention in Philadelphia, virtually every Democrat who attended was certain that Hillary Clinton was going to be the next president. Trump had won a fractured primary in unprecedented fashion, and there were plenty of prominent Republicans who wanted nothing to do with him. Ted Cruz spoke at the convention in Cleveland but didn't offer an endorsement. Other Republicans openly fretted about a landslide or even the destruction of the GOP itself. Clinton was going to win and it was only a matter of by how much.

Some of that same certainty, even smugness, was on the Republican side in the summer of 2024. Democrats, meanwhile, were behaving like the 2016 GOP, actively shirking their nominee. The Trump GOP was simultaneously savvier than it appeared and plenty toxic still. It had begun to eat away at the Democrats' working-class support in the same manner as other right-populist parties around the world. Republicans had denounced, repeatedly, mass migration, intuiting that Black and Spanish-speaking Americans did not feel much solidarity with immigrants illegally crossing the border. They had downplayed, as much as possible, their furious opposition to abortion, following the lead of Trump himself, who was against a federal abortion ban. They had ditched, in rhetoric, their supply-side dogma, embracing a vice presidential candidate in J. D. Vance who was skeptical of corporate power and willing to partner with Democrats to cap the price of insulin, regulate railroads, and halt corporate consolidation. Milton Friedman was nowhere near the Republican convention.

Still, the Republicans were not as dominant as they could be. In Milwaukee, as I imbibed the speeches and the harangues, I considered all that would have seemed deranged to the median voter. Peter Navarro ranted about the "lawfare jackals." Matt Gaetz rehashed the tired shtick about there having been only two genders when Trump was president. Ron DeSantis fumed, again, about the "woke mind virus." Just as so many Democrats throughout the 2010s and early 2020s behaved as if all politics was waged on Twitter, Republicans remained relentlessly online, convinced their obsessions over stolen elections, the alleged martyrs of January 6, and eliminating trans rights were shared by the broader electorate.

The loudest boos came at the mention of the name Alvin Bragg, the Manhattan Democratic district attorney who had successfully tried Trump. The greatest cheers, naturally, were for Trump himself, for his subdued appearances in the box, his light fist pumps, his waves to the crowd. Many of the speakers claimed, absurdly, that America was in far better shape four years ago, when the pandemic was raging (2020 was the new 2019, perhaps). On the convention floor, delegates waved signs that read "Mass Deportation Now!" in Trumpian font.

If there were no Electoral College, and Republicans had to become a majority party to win, they would have been incentivized to behave differently. In the meantime, it was thanks to Democratic frailty, not any grand yearning for the Trump project, that they had come so far.

Trump's speech at the convention was a meandering slurry; whatever pathos he found at the outset was buried under the typical, tedious fulminations against China, the illegals, and the Biden Democrats. As he blew past the hour mark, seemingly forgetting he was, in theory at least, trying to reach voters beyond his frenzied base in the convention, I realized he could only matter so much. Sure, Trump had survived an assassination attempt, and that was remarkable. The convention had built to his triumphant return, to his stampede to yet another Republican nomination. Literally no one inside the Fiserv Forum, I was certain, believed he wouldn't win in November.

As I made my way off the floor, and returned later to watch the balloons drop, I knew what was gnawing at me: All of this had been made possible by Democratic failure. Trump was there because the Democrats could not engineer effective, ordinary presidential campaigns; he was there, with Hulk Hogan and Kid Rock screeching, because Hillary Clinton ran one of the worst campaigns in modern American history. He was holding a commanding polling lead eight years later because the only choice open to the Democratic Party was between an eighty-one-year-old president who could not complete full sentences in a televised debate and a vice president who failed so badly in the 2020 primary that she never even competed in the Iowa caucuses. Trump was politically alive because Democrats throttled not one but two national primaries. Clinton, thanks to Barack Obama's intervention, was coronated in 2016, even though she had never won a truly competitive election and most voters were plainly revolted by the concept of a Clinton political dynasty. The only viable alternative was the septuagenarian Bernie Sanders, who took it upon himself to campaign despite the rancor of the Democratic establishment. It was then that Biden should have run. Instead, he was forced to wait until 2020, when he won because most Americans were tired of the pandemic and tired of Trump.

The implicit promise of that campaign was that Biden would be the bridge to the next generation of Democrats after defeating the Reality TV President. It turned out he very desperately wanted a second term, even as he slid into senility. His decision to run and forestall the possibility of an open primary among the large number of younger Democratic politicians who could have made a compelling case against Trump brought Americans to where they were that summer, befuddled and alienated by the political scene. Trump and Biden were terrifically unpopular.

Even after Biden withdrew from the campaign on July 21 and threw his support behind Kamala Harris, Trump still had his opening because the Democratic standard-bearer was going to be a California Democrat who nearly lost an attorney general's race there and had failed to distinguish herself in the Biden administration. Harris was the border czar, whatever that meant, and immigration was now one of Biden's great liabilities. At that point, she was a stronger candidate than Biden because she could go on television and speak cogently about Trump's failures. If the Democrats hadn't been so interested in squelching democracy, delegates would have huddled to settle on a process that could have opened the convention up and allowed for debates among candidates who would like to have been nominated. Why settle for Harris when the Democrats, for once, had a vibrant bench? They had the theoretical ability to nominate the governor of Michigan for president (Gretchen Whitmer) and the governor of Pennsylvania for vice president (Josh Shapiro), or flip it the other way. They could have looked to Raphael Warnock, the senator from Georgia who had successfully mobilized working-class Black voters in successive elections while courting suburban whites. They could have nominated Senator Mark Kelly of Arizona, who had won over independents despite reliably voting with the Democratic majority, and paired him with any of the aforementioned candidates. Roy Cooper, the North Carolina governor, was another intriguing choice, as was Wes Moore, the young Maryland governor. Gavin Newsom, the slick California governor, was lurking, of course, though

Republicans would have had a field day reminding voters that Newsom, Boris Johnson–style, flouted his own lockdown orders during the pandemic.

Give the elites their due: They recognized, belatedly, what a problem it was to have a decrepit Biden seek another term. They should had pressured him out of the race one or two years earlier, but they had learned not to fall prey to the sunk cost fallacy.

Trump's convention speech was a reminder that he was an undisciplined seventy-eight-year-old with a pathological inability to conceive of politics as anything other than a contest of petty grievances. He had been extraordinarily lucky in his life, and that fortune continued when it came to his Democratic opponents. He never would have won an election against Obama or Bill Clinton. He would have probably lost to the 2016 version of Biden. He had never won a popular vote. His rambling convention speech, in all its insipidness, was a reminder of what he would always lack, and where he'd forever fall short.

Done with the Republican convention and grateful to be bound for my hotel near Milwaukee airport, I wondered why Trump wanted all of this so badly. He would only get another four years as president. He was not, literally, the American Hitler, and he lacked the competency to cow the military, the FBI, the CIA, and the many Democrat-run states in order to establish whatever version of fascism MSNBC and *The New Republic* believed he was after. He longed for power and attention, and perhaps that was enough for him. Just as Democrats believed Trump would smash up the republic for good if he won, Republicans perceived the showdown in existential terms. Trump's base earnestly believed that another four years of Democratic rule would reduce the nation to some lawless, burnt-out wasteland, with Alvin Bragg and Dr. Fauci and the East Coast/West Coast Marxists teaming up to force through a Great Leap Forward, American-style.

I left the convention also convinced I had just spent several days in one of the wokest places in America. This might seem nonsensical or, to the nation's triumphant conservatives, an insult on the scale of declaring the Democrats won fair and square in 2020. These were, after all, the enlightened army of the anti-woke, the good doctors battling the *woke mind virus*, the rightful owners of libs everywhere. It was sunshine in the GOP every day—not a snowflake to be found anywhere.

Woke is social justice politics, and it's fair to say the modern Republican Party isn't terribly committed to that. But it's also a grievance politics. Identity and language obsessed, it rests on a foundation of victimhood and resists material analysis. Woke wars on the cultural terrain. Woke thins the discourse. Woke is one long screech into the night.

Woke was J. D. Vance insisting it was yucky words that got Donald Trump's skull nearly blown open. Woke was Kellyanne Conway boasting about all the women Trump had promoted during his campaign. Woke was treating Israel as an oppressed identity category. Woke was whining about the state of high school and college female sports. Woke was braying about Trump supporters being the most persecuted and marginalized in America; the 2024 RNC was intersectionality for Trump.

The discourse at the RNC was as free and open as any Robin DiAngelo struggle session. Suddenly, the Republicans were the woke scolds, the liberals returned to their old posture as the subversive joke tellers. Try cracking wise about Trump near a Trump delegate; try watching his soft skin redden. The discourse was so dumbed, so memetic, that the Trump Right would unleash the cancel culture mobs on anyone who dared speak ill of their Dear Leader, just as the campus left might have shouted at anyone who wore the wrong costume on Halloween. If there was one overriding message of the convention, it was that the Democrats were *mean*. They were *too mean* to Trump. They should stop playing dirty tricks and stop being mean. "Our family," Lara Trump despaired, had faced "tasteless and violent comments directed towards us on social media."

Tasteless and violent comments! *Couldn't these liberals just relax? Stop posting?!* The wokest of the woke might have been the crusaders against antisemitism, the Israel hawks who fit seamlessly with the evangelical Christian Zionists in the Republican coalition. The anti-woke free speech warriors wanted open discourse for everything except Israel. Israel was too precious, too special, its supporters too delicate to tolerate criticism in the public sphere. Ask Ben Shapiro. Ask Vance, who could somehow strike an isolationist posture on Ukraine but back the authorizing of endless military aid to another foreign nation that had done little, in recent years, to further American interests abroad. Combating antisemitism was the new anti-racism. Like Ibram X. Kendi, who popularized the concept of a pervasive, structural racism that could only be solved by a Manichean and implausible public policy—an anti-racist amendment that would make racial inequity "unconstitutional" over a "certain threshold"—the Republican anti-wokes obsessed with antisemitism believed it was everywhere all the time, worse than ever, worse than World War II, and could only be squelched by curtailing speech rights and nebulously policing hate crimes. Antisemitism could mean everything from literal Jew hatred (the actual definition) to believing that Israel should stop occupying the West Bank. Anyone who wanted to protest the State of Israel for the actions of its military would run into the new conservative scolds who equated language to violence and shed crocodile tears every time some twenty-three-year-old uttered "from the river to the sea" at a street protest. Nonviolent protest was not permissible because the words might hurt the feelings of a nuclear-armed American client state.

The RNC, like the old wokes, delighted in tokenism. There were Jewish tokens, of course, men in kippahs to thunder about the new Nazism visited upon us. There were Black and Latino tokens—Democrats and Republicans equally relish a good identity play—who arrived to tell you they were the blessed and all-seeing ones, their skin color offered up as a shield against the libs. Another anthem for the convention: *We're diverse too! Look, over there, a Black pastor who likes Trump! And over in the corner, to the right, isn't that Ben Carson? And Vivek what's-his-name? With a little more practice, we'll learn to how to pronounce it!* The convention floor itself was blindingly white. But so were all those women who bought *White Fragility* at their local independent bookstores.

"My message to my fellow Americans, those watching from across the country, is shouldn't we be governed by a party that is unafraid to debate ideas and come to the best solution?" Vance asked during his nomination speech. "That's the Republican Party of the next four years: united in our love for this country, and committed to free speech and the open exchange of ideas."

Unless those ideas included criticism of Israel or outright anti-Zionism. Or trans rights. Or any attempt to call it the Democratic Party and not *Democrat* Party, that infantile troll move of wretched grammar. Or quips about Trump himself—his bankruptcies, his infidelities, his deceptions, his lousy *Apprentice* ratings, his bloviating speeches, or his many White House failures. Try exchanging *those* ideas inside the convention. Try telling the furiously anti-immigrant GOP that it was the unchecked, borderless mass migration of the late 1800s and early 1900s that fueled the twentieth-century American renaissance, that our nation would have intellectually, culturally, and economically stagnated without this titanic surge of alien people. Tell them, in fact, that immigration self-selects for the most ambitious, the most motivated—that risking your life to enter a foreign nation makes you an ideal candidate for future citizenship, since you've already outworked most of the natives by simply showing up. Have that debate. I wasn't convinced the fulminating Republican libs could handle it. I thought they might get triggered. The RNC was a safe space, after all.

And there was a growing consensus, as the summer wore on, that Trump had made a mistake in picking Vance as his running mate. This had little to do, initially at least, with his politics. Most Republican politicians held social views that were far to the right of the median American; it was why Trump, for all his faults, forced the Republicans to engineer their most socially liberal party platform in many decades, effectively abandoning their crusades for a national abortion ban and a return to the pre-2015 status quo on same-sex marriage. The catch, as always, was that there were plenty of Republicans in Congress who *would* support a fifty-state abortion ban and not allowing any exceptions for rape and incest. They may get their shot one day. But for now, it was Trump's party, and Trump was a thrice-married philanderer who would appoint all the right-wing judges the Christian nationalists demanded but wouldn't jeopardize his election prospects by running on whatever Franklin Graham or Bob Vander Plaats truly desired.

Vance now resided in this camp: a Republican whose views on gender and sexuality damaged Trump. They wholly negated how Vance had been able to triangulate Democrats from the left on economics, delivering a convention speech that echoed Bernie Sanders and Sherrod Brown on the need to check corporate power in America. Theoretically, Vance was Trump's best pick for vice president because he was a cunning thirty-nine-year-old who grasped why right-populist parties across the world have found so much success. You demonize immigrants while embracing left-wing economics; you protect the social safety net while braying about blood and soil. You kill Milton Friedman and Friedrich von Hayek for good. It's not much more complicated than that.

But Trump, and the Republicans, had a problem. Vance was, very clearly, a beta.

For those who don't spend most of their days online, like Vance plainly did, a beta is a loser, a chump, a weakling. A beta falls in line. A beta is the opposite of an alpha. The alpha is the leader, the kingpin; the alpha swaggers. Vance, obviously, wasn't a loser in any conventional sense. He was a millionaire, a best-selling author, and a United States senator. As he'd remind you repeatedly, he was also married with children. He had all the armaments of traditional success.

And yet—and Trump, if pressed, would have probably admitted this privately—Vance was a beta.

Alphahood can't be bought. And betahood can't be readily chased away.

I began to think this as I watched Vance, in a perplexing fundraising video, show off all the junk food he won't eat at Republican events. "They've got a ton of crap for you to drink and eat," a slimmed-down Vance, in a suit and tie, said to the camera. "Free bottles of Diet Mountain Dew, about a dozen Snicks, a bag of chips. If I ate even half this stuff, of course, I balloon up like crazy."

Vance went on to ask viewers to donate to the Trump campaign. It was one of the stranger segues I had seen, and it was a reminder of what I felt when I watched Vance at the RNC—ideology and politics aside, he was absent charisma. He was not born with it, and he would not discover it on the campaign trail. If his biography was, in a way, shockingly similar to Barack Obama's—an Ivy League law degree, a rise to fame through a zeitgeist-defining memoir, and a brief Senate stint from a Midwestern state—he lacked all of Obama's verve and magnetism. And Trump's, too. It was inarguable that Trump, with his genius for hoarding attention, knew how to put on a good show.

Vance had come to remind me of another Republican, one who was ultimately doomed: Jeb Bush.

Bush and Vance diverged greatly on political substance. Vance excoriated the Iraq War that the Bush family made possible. Bush extolled Reaganomics. He was representative of the old-line Republican establishment that Vance and his ilk have so furiously opposed. Bush was the past and Vance was the future.

But Jeb, for reasons never very clear, babbled on and on about his weight loss. He wanted you to know he was ditching starch and refined sugars. He snacked on almonds. During a meeting with veterans at an IHOP, a thick stack of pancakes was placed in front of him with a second platter of eggs, bacon, and hash browns. The veterans gladly ate. Bush left his breakfast untouched, to the disappointment of the restaurant's staff.

There is nothing wrong with being healthy. Vance and Bush wanted to be slim and live long lives. What set them apart from both the slovenly Trump and the effortlessly svelte Obama was the performative nature of their snacking. They believed that, somehow, they were winning votes this way, that loudly talking up the dangers of carbs and snack foods would make them appealing to someone, somewhere.

Beta move.

But this awkwardness, on its own, wasn't Vance's major liability. It was more symptom than cause—his tin ear for what resonates in politics—and the real problem had to do with what had gotten attention in the media of late. This was his 2021 crack about "childless cat ladies" running the country and his inability, in an interview with Megyn Kelly, to apologize or at least explain it away. "Obviously, it was a sarcastic comment. I've got nothing against cats," he said, before whining that the media was "focusing so much on the sarcasm and not on the substance of what I actually said."

And this was the substance: "It's not a criticism of people who don't have children. I explicitly said in my remarks . . . this is not about criticizing people who for various reasons don't have kids. This is about criticizing the Democratic Party for becoming anti-family and anti-child."

Trump, as the critic B. D. McClay pointed out, was too savvy for this stuff. Or, at the very minimum, he was too offline for it. A father of five, he had never gone around lashing the childless. For one, it would never have occurred to him to do so—the obsession with natalism is very twenty-first century, very of the internet—and he understood, dimly at least, that there are a lot of childless people who vote. The Republican convention, when not sanctifying Trump, was an exercise in promoting the GOP as the "big tent" party, one that could ape the rhetorical quirks of the social justice left. Cat ladies and cat men, all are welcome.

Vance's problem might have been that he was born in 1984, which meant he'd grown up with an internet connection, and his politics were mediated through Reddit, podcasts, and peculiar blogs. Vance had made an idol of Curtis Yarvin. Have you *seen* Curtis Yarvin? Trump, in his heyday, used to hang out at Studio 54. Do you think Curtis Yarvin could have got into Studio 54? Do you think Trump would let Curtis Yarvin come within five hundred yards of any of his gold-plated shlock? Donald Trump Jr. would—he loves Vance—but

Junior is a rich-kid try-hard, who grew up imbibing the myth of his father and realizing, slowly, he would never be that exciting or notable to that many people. Trump, at one point many decades ago, did look a little like Robert Redford. His son, not so much.

Junior and Vance could bond over their betahood.

Mike Pence made a great deal of sense for Trump because evangelical Christians had to be convinced that the vessel for their hopes and dreams was a New Yorker living in biblical sin. Pence was solemn, steely, and mildly terrifying. *The Handmaid's Tale* memes were meant for him. Vance is the doughy keyboard warrior made real, the master of subreddits who is surprised to learn meatspace isn't governed by the same rules. He won a Senate race in spite of himself; he ran behind the other Republicans in deep-red Ohio, and struggled for months to put away his Democratic opponent, Tim Ryan. He wrote a decent memoir that was extraordinarily well-timed and marketed wonderfully by his publisher. He befriended Peter Thiel, who made him rich. He convinced Trump Jr. he was worth an endorsement from Trump Sr. in an Ohio primary he otherwise would not have won. And he limped over the finish line in a state that might never vote for a Democrat as president again. Now, on the national stage, he was exposed, boasting the lowest favorability rating of any vice presidential candidate in memory. Even Sarah Palin had a demented star quality. Vance, even as vice president, would only burn so bright.

3

Biden

What was worse, truly? A media and political class that actively lied to the public? Or a media and political class that was so inept, ignorant, and cloistered that it failed to recognize the reality in front of them?

I had been fielding many questions that boiled down to some version of *how did this happen?* through the crisis summer of 2024, shortly before Joe Biden suddenly announced he would be the first president since Lyndon Johnson to forego running for another term. A quick and dirty answer blamed our presidential system, which treats its presidents like kings and offers little in the way of accountability or counterbalance for an executive that wants to keep pushing forward. This wasn't parliament. If Biden wanted to run for president badly enough, he'd run. Who was going to stop him?

Absent the mechanisms of parliament or the old-world political bosses who could persuade presidents to stand down, all that was left was public pressure. And while every available public poll showed most voters were uncomfortable with the idea of a president serving until he was eighty-six, polls alone weren't enough. The respondents weren't marching in the streets. They were registering their disdain to pollsters and getting on with their lives.

It was up to the media and the Democratic political class. For at least two years, the latter cajoled or bullied the former into submission. Both earnestly believed a lie or didn't; they knew Biden was diminished but argued otherwise, in the hope that he could win and none of this would matter. They made a calculation that the 2020 playbook could be rerun again, that Donald Trump was too noxious and that a doddering, befuddled president wouldn't bother Americans as much as an oft-unhinged and now convicted criminal. They might have been right or catastrophically wrong. That was the wager they made.

The June 27 clash between Biden and Trump—the first time a current and former president had collided in a televised debate—would turn out to be the most consequential presidential debate of the modern era, maybe ever. Here the Biden Lie was fully exposed for millions to see: he could not finish his sentences or speak coherently. He could not stand up against Trump, or anyone. He mumbled about how he "beat Medicare," and fumbled basic facts. Biden's closest aides, who had cosseted him from the public and berated anyone who questioned the president's fitness, were exposed for what they were: rank enablers on course to hand the White House back to Trump.

The conclusion of the debate kicked off one of the more extraordinary string of weeks in the twenty-first century. Major liberal pundits, so smugly supportive of Biden for so long—so utterly convinced that reasonable questions about his age were a right-wing disinformation operation—had now turned on him. They had seen enough. Matt Yglesias wanted Biden gone, Tom Friedman wanted Biden gone, Nick Kristof wanted Biden gone. Some practiced introspection, others did not. There wasn't much of a reckoning over why it took one debate to convince them of what had been obvious for at least two years. This was the same president who had said, multiple times, that his son who died of brain cancer had actually died in Iraq. This was the same president who, at a public event, had called out to a congresswoman who was already dead. This was a president who had even declined a pre-game interview on Super Bowl Sunday, a tradition dating back decades and one of the rare times, in the modern age, anyone can address a mass audience of Democrats, Republicans, and independents.

As Biden tottered, I recalled my experience of writing, in 2022, that he should quit while he's ahead and permit an open primary to replace him. Unhinged Democrats sent me death threats. Others tut-tutted that I was doing the bidding of Republicans, undercutting a great man who plainly was *entitled* to run again. My piece, published in *New York* magazine, made clear there was much I admired about the Biden policy record. With a 50–50 Senate majority, he was able to oversee enormous, consequential investments in infrastructure, green energy, and semiconductor chips, and make other much-needed reforms, like capping the price of insulin and permitting Medicare to negotiate the cost of prescription drugs. Biden could, absolutely, declare himself a successful president on the domestic front, arguably outstripping the man he served with for eight years, Barack Obama.

None of that mattered, though, when he was obviously slipping into senility. It didn't matter that he was the only Democrat, until then, who had beaten Trump, or that some Democrats still felt intense loyalty to him. Members of Congress began calling for him to exit the race. Nancy Pelosi, attuned to the polls and still fretting congressional majorities in her eighties, rallied Biden-skeptical Democrats, applying pressure on him, in phone calls and meetings, to leave the race. The most devastating blow for Biden, though, may not have been Pelosi's turn or the growing reluctance of Chuck Schumer and Hakeem Jeffries, the Democratic congressional leaders, to back him in public.

It may have been the extraordinarily wealthy—the Hollywood left and the East Coast financiers—who played a decisive role in toppling Biden. Perhaps no billionaire had clung closer to Biden than Jeffrey Katzenberg, who made his billions producing *The Lion King* and *Shrek*. Katzenberg was both the Hollywood Democratic bag man and a frequent White House guest, roaming the West Wing and dispensing advice. He once traveled with Biden to Camp David to help him prepare a national address. Just two weeks before Biden debated Trump on television, the *New York Times* published a piece calling Katzenberg Biden's "secret weapon" against Trump, reporting that he had rallied leading politicians and Hollywood glitterati alike, including George Clooney and Julia Roberts, to Biden's side. If anyone had questions about Biden's fitness, Katzenberg was the man to assuage their fears.

"He was like, 'Trust me. And if you don't trust me, trust, but verify. Come with me and see for yourself and engage with the president,'" Gavin Newsom, the California governor, told the *Times*. "He really was instrumental in getting people off the sidelines and getting them to dive headfirst into this campaign."

But Katzenberg, in the hours after the June 27 debate, seemed like the fairy-tale denizen who had watched his lithe princess transform into a scabrous ogre. He was done with Biden, and appeared to play a role in an opinion piece Clooney published in the *Times* calling for Biden to withdraw. The Clooney piece was most serious because he was speaking for the spigot—if Clooney was through, so were all the liberal millionaires and billionaires floating through Hollywood. Throughout the Republican National Convention, which came in the third week of July, Biden aides had to keep tamping down (true) reports that he was soon finished, that delegates were deserting him.

Unlike Lyndon Johnson in 1968, Biden did not do a sober reading of the polls or respond, in some fashion, to the will of the people. Johnson had to run in a genuine Democratic primary and it was a near-loss to the anti-war Eugene McCarthy in New Hampshire that sealed his fate; with the Vietnam War raging, he was simply too unpopular to continue, and knew it. Biden, meanwhile, only needed to win a sham primary against a little-known congressman from Minnesota, Dean Phillips, and Marianne Williamson, a perennial political candidate and spiritual guru. The Democratic establishment had successfully pressured every viable contender to stand aside. Unlike Johnson, Biden simply did not *believe* the polls as the year wore on. He was falling further behind Trump and it didn't matter. His aides, like former chief of staff Ron Klain, would take to social media to badger journalists who thought otherwise. They dismissed Democratic critics of Biden as "bedwetters." And their great hubris led them into the final trap, the June debate, which Biden forced upon Trump. Biden would have ended up the nominee had he simply debated his opponent in September and October like all recent presidents had done.

He survived into July because the media and pundit class had been so gullible and willfully blind. They could not muster the observational fortitude to understand what was obvious to millions of voters, to anyone who applied the median view to this political situation. There was the bare fact of a man in his eighties trying to perform the most demanding job in all the world. There was the bare fact of *this* man doing it—someone who was, mentally at least, no longer as fit as other politicians of the same generation. Had Bernie Sanders somehow won in 2020, he would have been facing, with good reason, the same age-related scrutiny as Biden. But Sanders, a year older, was far more capable of debating Trump than Biden was. He had all of his mental faculties. Watching him give a speech or an interview made that clear: He'd never blurt out, as if in a medicinal daze, *we beat Medicare.* In 2022, I had interviewed Elizabeth Holtzman, the former congresswoman who, in her eighties, was trying to make a political comeback. Holtzman, older than Biden, had retained her sharpness and mental acuity. She could easily recall facts. She completed sentences. She was capable of going back to Washington.

What did these pundits, journalists, and politicians *see* in Biden? How were they so blinded? So devoid of basic bullshit detection? These are questions historians will be left to pick over for decades. Future generations may be befuddled by us. This was a crisis Democrats had absolutely earned.

Its origin lay in Biden, of course, who had dreamed of being president since his election to the Senate at twenty-nine and found himself, at seventy-eight, finally entering the Oval Office after beating Trump in the pandemic year of 2020. Biden had not explicitly promised to be a one-term president—he was too ambitious and cagey for that—but he had talked, on the trail, of being a "bridge" to the next generation of Democrats. The highest turnout election in America since women were granted the right to vote brought millions to the polls who were hoping, above all else, Biden could beat Trump. This was how he ultimately crushed his rivals in the 2020 Democratic primary; the aforementioned Sanders, Massachusetts Senator Elizabeth Warren, and Pete Buttigieg, who would end up Biden's transportation secretary, could not forcefully make the same electability arguments. Biden had bolstered Barack Obama's tickets and the Obama nostalgia clung to him. He was the man of the hour.

And he had started, not long after his election, trying to engineer a primary that would somehow forestall what was coming for him at the end of his only term.

In December 2022, the thirty-odd members of the Democratic Party's rules and bylaws committee filed into the Omni Shoreham, the glittering resort hotel that once hosted Franklin D. Roosevelt's inaugural ball. All of the attendees, many of them gray-haired habitués of the rubber-chicken circuit, knew they had come to Washington to hash out, after months of debate, what the presidential-primary calendar would look like come 2024.

The order in which the states vote has defined American politics since the 1970s, when Jimmy Carter rocketed to the presidency on the strength of his performance in the Iowa caucuses. Always Iowa first, then New Hampshire—which zealously guarded its status as the first-in-the-nation primary, luring all future presidents to the rickety diner back rooms and high school gymnasiums of the flinty Northern state. Biden performed terribly in each of those contests in 2020, hitting his stride only in larger states with fewer white voters. It was now understood that the curious caucus system—voters clustering on cold church and library floors to choose candidates—needed to be retired, particularly after Iowa failed to tally the vote in a timely manner.

So Iowa would be demoted, as would tolerance for any kind of caucus. New Hampshire, perhaps, would vote first, alongside Nevada with its increasing Latino population.

In the event, however, the co-chair of the rules and bylaws committee—and the grandson of Franklin Roosevelt—made a different announcement.

"I move a resolution, which will be displayed on the screen," James Roosevelt Jr. said, "which grants waivers to Rule 12-A, conditional upon the outlined stipulations for a state-run primary in South Carolina on Feb. 3, 2024; New Hampshire and Nevada on Feb. 6; Georgia on Feb. 13 . . ."

The room offered no immediate public reaction to the legalese. But privately, some members were astounded. "Everyone was shocked," one told me, speaking on the condition of anonymity to avoid antagonizing the White House. "We would have to vote for it anyway, because the feeling was you're either with the president or against him."

A few members of the Democratic National Committee had known what was coming—but only because Biden administration officials called them on the phone mere hours after Biden himself sent a letter to the rules and bylaws committee, on the first day of December, outlining his demand for a primary calendar that ensured that "voters of color have a voice in choosing our nominee much earlier in the process and throughout the entire early window." Biden called Black voters the "backbone" of the party, though he didn't specifically mention South Carolina in his letter. It was left to his aides to tell the top-ranking DNC members, including Roosevelt, that South Carolina was the new first-in-the-nation primary. It had been decreed, and so it would be done.

As chairman of the DNC, Jaime Harrison had strained to play mediator between angered state Democrats and a White House that expected fealty from the national organization. Harrison was sanguine about the fortunes of his party. He was not troubled, throughout 2022 and 2023 and even 2024, about Biden's age. Nor did he fret his party's declining share among many demographic groups, especially Latino voters and those without college degrees, or a dire Senate map, where Democratic incumbents in Montana, Ohio, and West Virginia were all fated to fall, plunging Democrats into an indefinite minority.

In Harrison's office at DNC headquarters, which looks out on the dome of the Capitol, there hangs a portrait of Biden with Jim Clyburn, the octogenarian South Carolina congressman whose endorsement and championing of Biden in 2020 was credited with rescuing his candidacy. Displayed over Harrison's desk is a vintage sign for Ron Brown, who in 1989 became the first Black chairman of the DNC. Brown and Clyburn were both heroes to Harrison, who was Clyburn's intern and, later, his director of floor operations when the congressman served as majority whip. A lucrative private-sector career followed as a lobbyist at the Podesta Group. With Clyburn's blessing, he became chairman of the South Carolina Democratic Party.

Harrison then ran a high-profile, extremely expensive, and very unsuccessful campaign in 2020 for the Senate seat held by Lindsey Graham. Now Clyburn's protégé headed a DNC that had put their home state, where Harrison still lived with his family, quite literally first.

Harrison insisted that Clyburn never advocated for South Carolina as the very first state, only for it to retain its status as the first of the Southern states. "I think, for him, he always wanted South Carolina—and I felt the same way—we enjoyed and took a lot of pride in being the first in the South," Harrison told me in 2023, sitting beneath that portrait. "People thought early on, *Oh God, Jaime's the chair of the DNC, so therefore he's going to put his finger on the scale for South Carolina.* And everybody will tell you, I was evenhanded in this. The only thing that I wanted was that South Carolina would *remain*, because I think it's earned its spot as an early state." But South Carolina, of course, moved up, and Harrison was thrilled.

> National Geographic said that 90 percent of African Americans can trace one of their ancestors to South Carolina. In our primary, 50 to 60 percent of the people who vote in the Democratic primary will be Black folks. Think about how powerful this is, that the descendants of those enslaved people will be the very first people in this country to determine the most powerful person on the face of this planet. That's transformative.

A few dissidents in the DNC, made up of New Hampshirites and some Iowans, progressives, and union members, saw it differently: Biden was elevating a state that a Democratic presidential candidate hadn't carried since 1976. Beyond Clyburn, there were few Democrats of note in South Carolina, and the state had the lowest percentage of union membership in America. Progressive candidates could, cycle after cycle, meet a wall of opposition there.

The persistent quandary, which no version of the primary calendar could resolve, was how to account for the various long-range challenges of the Democratic Party. A first-in-the-nation South Carolina primary lends Black moderates, a pivotal Democratic constituency, the kind of clout that many believe they deserve. White rural voters—the sort who need to be courted in

Iowa and New Hampshire—have not proved loyal to the Democratic brand. But there are only so many of them that Democrats can afford to lose in a general election. New Hampshire, which Biden carried by less than ten points in 2020, was not guaranteed to be eternally blue.

On my 2023 visit, a wall in the DNC lobby featured portraits honoring the highest-ranking Democrats: Biden; Vice President Harris; Schumer, the majority leader; the head of the Senate's campaign arm, Senator Gary Peters of Michigan; Jaime Harrison. But the wall seemed to have been frozen in pre-midterm 2022: Nancy Pelosi, not Hakeem Jeffries, the new House minority leader, had a portrait on the wall, as did Sean Patrick Maloney, the New York Democrat who led the Democratic Congressional Campaign Committee (DCCC). Not only was Maloney no longer the DCCC chair, he was not in Congress at all. He had lost his re-election bid, helping to cost Democrats their majority.

The DNC raises and spends titanic sums of money on organizing and messaging for political contests: more than $300 million over the course of 2021 and 2022, leading up to the midterms. The committee is a constellation of various interests—activists, wealthy donors, state party chairs—that is more fractious than its Republican counterpart because of the sheer number of individuals who make up the 483-member national committee, which far outstrips the 168-member RNC. The Republican Party has had its own ideological struggles, but the once-insurgent Trump wing has come to largely command party business, and all Republicans there have fallen in line.

When a Democratic president is in the White House, the DNC chair is more empowered foot soldier than swaggering executive. The president handpicks a chair who is expected to do whatever it is the president wants, which usually boils down to burnishing his reputation and preparing for re-election. If, historically, Democratic presidents aren't ignoring the DNC altogether—many a party leader, over the last seventy years, has trudged to the White House with a grand plan for the downballot that was dismissed out of hand—they are actively predatory, setting up rival organizations to siphon off donations and resources.

Most observers might imagine this dynamic impacts the RNC and DNC equally. Why would a Republican president, invested with the same sort of world-historical significance and ego, be any different than a Democratic president? But, historically, they *are*, argued Daniel Galvin, a political science professor at Northwestern University. "The basic difference between the two parties is that Republican presidents—at least starting with Eisenhower and going through George W. Bush—made investing in their party organization a priority," Galvin told me. "Democrats have always been behind in that regard."

For much of the second half of the twentieth century, Democrats enjoyed durable, seemingly unbreakable majorities at the congressional and state levels. Even when Republican contenders like Dwight Eisenhower, Richard Nixon, and Ronald Reagan won dominant victories, Democrats kept a stranglehold on Congress and a large advantage over the GOP when it came to the number of Americans who identified with their party. Some of this was due to the legacy of the New Deal—Franklin Roosevelt's presidency lasted into a fourth term and created widely popular programs like Social Security—and some of it sprung from the Democrats' own peculiar coalition, left over from the nineteenth century: southern segregationists, rural populists, and northern liberals all belonged to the same party. Democrats, in addition, could count on the backing of large labor unions, robust urban political machines, and activist organizations that consistently whipped the vote for their candidates.

All of this meant that Democratic presidents, from John F. Kennedy onward, had little use for the actual DNC. They wanted the party to promote their policies and do little else. Some, like Lyndon Johnson, actively raided funds that could have been used for party-building initiatives. The Democratic state parties themselves began to wither in the 1970s and '80s, as each successive Democratic president took for granted their congressional majorities. Jimmy Carter neglected the party as much as Kennedy and Johnson did. Bill Clinton, until his second term—following a Republican wave that broke the forty-year lock Democrats held on the

House—was no different than any of his Democratic predecessors.

By then, the urban machines were desiccated, unions were on a steep decline, and Republicans were decades ahead of the Democrats when it came to the intricacies of party-building: regularly training campaign managers and state chairs, recruiting candidates, assembling a national voter file, and registering and microtargeting voters. Each Republican president had been deeply invested in the project of crafting a majority for their own party, since one always seemed to be just out of each. By the 1990s, the RNC was unquestionably a vibrant party entity, well-versed in schooling operatives and bolstering the state organizations.

The DNC, meanwhile, was not much more than a shell organization, tasked mostly with raising cash for the president and planning the national convention. Each president seemed to leave it in crippling debt.

Unlike the RNC, which has a half-century tradition of buttressing downballot candidates, the DNC has only done this work intermittently. After Trump's defeat in 2020, it was left to independent organizations like the States Project and Run for Something to help recruit and fund candidates for legislative and county-level campaigns. "It would be much, much better if there was a unified way of engaging with these races," said Amanda Litman, Run for Something's co-founder. "It's a problem the right doesn't have."

The DNC naturally transfers many millions of dollars to the campaign committees of the Senate and the House, which are tasked with contesting costly seats every two years. Super PACs gobble up plenty of donations, too. Rather than attempt the painstaking work of bolstering or resurrecting a local Democratic organization, wealthy donors can cut large checks to PACs and campaign arms.

The Obama era was particularly cataclysmic for Democrats on the state level. Republicans dominated a redistricting process that safeguarded their legislative majorities for much of the next decade; by 2016, the last full year of Obama's presidency, Democrats had full control of just seven states. Even after the Democrats' triumphant 2022 midterm, Republicans controlled twenty-eight state legislatures to the Democrats' nineteen. And it's these state legislatures that decide much of the policy—taxes, education, transit—that impact everyday American life.

The DNC suffered under Obama, in part because he created his own political group, Organizing for Action, outside the aegis of the party. The group built a parallel structure that hoovered up donor cash. State party chairs were livid, believing that the group, which focused chiefly on the promotion of Obama's policy agenda, deprived them of attention and dollars. Heading into 2020, the Democratic presidential contenders, including Biden, pledged not to create another extra-party organ.

Almost a decade before she became a Trump cabinet member, Tulsi Gabbard was a vice chair of the DNC. A young congresswoman from Hawaii, Gabbard said she experienced "elitism" at the DNC that demonstrated a "disconnect" from voters elsewhere. Her ultimate disenchantment would come when she decided to support Sanders for president in 2016 and believed DNC leadership was trying to actively undercut him instead of remaining neutral in the primary, as they professed.

"I agreed to be a vice chair because I had some idealism thinking I could go in and actually affect the direction of the Democratic Party. And over time, especially as we headed into that 2016 election, I found that the answer was 'no,'" Gabbard told me. "The constant refrain I heard from folks in different states across the country is the DNC likes to raise a lot of money off of us but they don't pay attention to us until a few weeks before the election."

Cedric Richmond, the former Alabama congressman, left his job in 2022 as a senior White House advisor to take on a similar, if nebulous, role at the DNC. Richmond earned $20,850 each month for what was described as "political strategy and consulting" in Federal Election Commission filings. His monthly fee, equating to a $250,000 annual salary, outstripped even what Harrison, as chairman, made. (Harrison's biweekly salary of around $7,800 prorated to just over $200,000.)

Richmond appeared on television as a Biden

surrogate and helps fundraise for the DNC. He then was busy with other matters, advocating for the Federal Communication Commission to allow a New York hedge fund to purchase a local TV broadcaster, creating a new conglomerate. Labor unions and anti-monopolists were against the deal, while Richmond, along with leaders like Rev. Al Sharpton, hoped to create America's largest minority-owned media company. Ultimately, the merger didn't go through.

Another vice chair of the DNC was Henry Muñoz III, who has also been the party's finance chair in the past. DNC staff were less eager to discuss Muñoz, a prodigious fundraiser and activist in the Latino community. The *Daily Beast*'s Will Bredderman reported in 2023 that Muñoz has earned more than $30 million as a consultant to SOMOS Community Care, a state-funded healthcare nonprofit catering to poor and working-class New Yorkers. Muñoz, however, possesses no apparent healthcare expertise or a medical degree. (He did, however, have a relationship with Dr. Ramon Tallaj, SOMOS's chairman. Tallaj was an early donor to Latino Victory, the PAC Muñoz founded.)

These kinds of donors were on my mind as I arrived at the Democratic National Convention in Chicago in August 2024. On the second night, I stood with many hundreds of human beings in Ride App Zone Lot 35, waiting for a car to come and get me. We were all, like befuddled toddlers, squinting at our phones, summoning cars that would not come. We had our credentials slung dutifully around our necks because we had just come from the United Center, where the Democrats had finished night two of their convention. Since none of us, apparently, were staying at the DNC-designated hotels—they've got chartered buses for that—we were stuck in the lot, beleaguered masses trying against all odds to escape. When your driver was within several minutes of Ride App Zone Lot 35, you were supposed to text them to ask them for their lane number, where they would then appear to whisk you away. With six minutes to go, I texted my Uber driver to tell me his lane number when he arrived. A minute later, he canceled the ride.

Seeing the snarl of traffic, the delirium of bodies, I did not blame him.

I joked, on another platform that rocketed to great prominence in the 2010s, that I would disrupt all of this chaos with a new technology called "Taxi Stand," which I would bring to Silicon Valley and make $10 billion from. As the night wore on, I considered whether that was really such a joke, if this was where the titanic tech revolutions of the 2010s had got us—thronged in a parking lot, clenching dying smartphones, treating the taxicab like Godot.

Because, of course, this was a problem that got solved many, many decades ago. In large cities with large crowds, there were taxi companies and taxi drivers, and they lined up curbside near arenas and stadiums to take people home. No phones were required. Instead, people would come to a designated point, stand in line, and depart one-by-one or two-by-two, or however large their party might be, into the taxis idling at the curb. Chicago has a taxi industry, but I imagine, like taxi industries everywhere, it is ailing and perhaps on the way to being dead. Milwaukee, where the 2024 Republican National Convention was held, did not seem to have taxis at all, or at least cars roaming the streets that you could flag down. When I asked a convention worker where a taxi stand might be, he reacted like I was inquiring after Western Union's telegraph office. In Chicago, I hoped one might exist, a simple place where I could stand in line and eventually get a cab. Instead, I found the Ride App Zone.

Eventually, an Uber driver stuck with me but told me to *leave* the Ride App Zone and walk several blocks away. I struggled to find him, on the corner of Ashland and Madison, traffic snaking in all four directions. But he waited, and was kindly when I finally located his Toyota near a bus stop. His name was Rodrigo and he told me drivers were canceling when they saw a potential customer was in the Ride App Zone. "It's too hard to get there," he said, and he was right. Since the DNC had designated no extended curbside for cars to quickly take people away, there was no straightforward way for rideshare drivers to easily reach the lot or the "lanes." It was a catastrophe, and it was probably going to be my fate for the rest of the week.

In 2019, I wrote an essay on the Uber presidency, my intention being to link Donald Trump to the rideshare behemoth. It was a clever premise, and one I stand by, since Trump's political career and Uber's success were built alike on bombast, deception, and law-breaking. Uber, until recently, never turned a profit, and was able to burn up capital in acquiring ever-greater gobs thanks to the market share it won through its blitzkrieg of major American cities. In New York, where I live and work, Uber expanded exponentially, unconstrained by a medallion system that was created to limit congestion on the roadways. Uber triumphed, in part, because the taxi industry made a great foil, being filled with corruption and its own slumlord class of medallion-hoarders. But the drivers of the yellow taxis themselves were working-class immigrants, and they saw the investments they made in their futures come to nothing; driving a taxi in the 2010s was like owning a house in the latter half of the 2000s, or maybe worse. Some taxi drivers committed suicide. Uber kept growing, even as its business model only made sense as long as interest rates stayed at zero and venture capitalists were happy to pump ever more cash into its coffers, content that the company had sufficiently saturated the market to make itself indispensable. In the twentieth century, corporations had to turn a profit to expand; Uber grew as it lost money. And since the company's labor costs were so low—the drivers were contractors—its expansion could continue apace.

In America, Uber has won. They had first-mover advantage in relation to the app technology, and now they are every city's taxi industry. New York's streets are tremendously congested, and the sheer number of vehicles locals and tourists summon on their phones to take rides that could be made via bus or subway has played a definitive role. There is a parallel universe where a strong regulatory state forced Uber to follow local law and grow gradually, and where local taxis were outfitted with app technology. Today, yellow taxis in New York have an app, but it's Uber (and Lyft) who get the calls because they were allowed to defy all existing vehicle regulations and flood the streets for a pivotal stretch in the early 2010s, when all new tech was venerated and the smartphone was supposed to be liberatory.

This was Barack Obama's America. Obama, as always, delivered a stirring speech at the Democratic National Convention, and his wife's might have been even better. They flayed Trump and elicited many rousing cheers and chants. Michelle Obama proved she could have had the Democratic nomination if she'd wanted it, but she didn't need it, since life is better on the outside, where no one is sullying you in the media and there are millions to be made. The speeches were gauzy and ill-defined on the policy front, offering little more than certain warm vibrations. No one truly knows what a Kamala Harris presidency would have looked like. But we know, for all his oratory genius, what an Obama presidency resembled, and it was one where the tech titans were sanctified and the revolving door was thrown wide open between the White House and the richest corporations in the world. Jay Carney, Obama's press secretary, scurried off to Amazon. David Plouffe, one of the Obama campaign wizards, became Uber's missionary to the world and later a Facebook employee, before returning to work for Harris after his exile during the Biden years. Eric Holder, the Attorney General, went to Airbnb, and Lisa Jackson, Obama's Environmental Protection Agency head, joined Apple. Dozens of less celebrated Obama staffers flooded Silicon Valley, trading on their federal expertise to make far more money while ensuring that those who remained in government treated Big Tech kindly. "There is an undeniable appeal to the growth and excitement of the tech industry—especially when contrasted to working in a large bureaucracy with a lot of rules and a lot of reasons to say no," Nick Sinai, former US Deputy Chief Technology Officer and a venture capitalist with Insight Venture Partners, told CNN in 2016.

Those *rules* Sinai lamented safeguard consumers and curtail abuse; had they been applied aggressively in the Obama era, they might have prevented the curdling of the internet and the broader tech that we are now forced to interact with daily. There wasn't a corporate merger the Obama administration didn't celebrate or at least permit with little tangible resistance. Facebook forestalled its eventual oblivion by gobbling up Instagram and WhatsApp. Live Nation and Ticketmaster merged, damaging the music industry and punishing online ticket-buyers. During Obama's presidency, Google acquired more than 150 companies unchallenged—including Waze for a mere $1.3 billion—and developed a monopoly over search and GPS navigation that has gradually degraded both. It would be an exaggeration to say that technology is so rapacious, sinister, and *inefficient* today—search results spamified, social media polluted—because Obama was president, but his administration plainly did nothing to head off this peculiar, numbing hell we are all subjected to on a second-by-second basis. Even if Obama didn't make this happen, he *let* it happen. Few in the Chicago convention hall seriously thought about that.

Joe Biden, to his credit, installed an antitrust regime, beginning with Lina Khan, his chair of the Federal Trade Commission. The Biden Justice Department successfully sued Google. Pete Buttigieg, Biden's transportation secretary, even blocked an airline merger. There was a budding school of thought, fueled by the early mania around Harris, that this economic populism represented a wrong turn. Centrist pundits like Jonathan Chait yearned for the old world, when the center-left and Big Tech hugged each other tight and never let go. If Biden is so unpopular, they intimated, it *must* be because of his policies. The people want their government officials to get rich in the private sector again! Except, of course, almost all of Biden's falling fortunes were tied to his age, and his obvious inability to campaign aggressively against Trump. Inflation and immigration were dogging him, but had he been seventy-one, or simply in possession of the cognition of fellow octogenarians like Bernie Sanders and Nancy Pelosi, he could have forged forward and built the kind of polling lead Harris initially enjoyed. But the voters, rightly, were uncomfortable with Biden, who had visibly declined before their eyes. They were not asking for Harris to purge the trustbusters and tech skeptics. Most probably they weren't aware of what was happening in the Biden administration anyway.

Obama is a curious Democratic Party kingpin. He exerts enough influence to determine the course of national primaries, and his wife is wildly popular. There is no single policy Michelle Obama is yoked to, or any particular vision—the attraction lies simply in her demeanor and natural charisma, her approachable celebrity, and she is probably the most beloved first lady since Jackie Kennedy. Obama himself has been resuscitated after eight years of Trump and Biden, two elderly men who made history in all the wrong ways. As the first Black president, Obama is a special vehicle for nostalgia, especially as millennials slide into middle age. Even in his sixties, with his hair gone white, he embodies youth—had John F. Kennedy lived, he would have been potent in the same way, a callback for the generation of 1960 who revered him so, haunting, in the flesh, Nixon and Ford and Carter and Reagan. Obama's failures have been sanded away. He can, forever, be the Obama of 2008, *Yes We Can*, the singular politician who drove college students and young professionals into a sort of frenzy that was almost metaphysical and will probably never be witnessed again.

4

Social Justice

There has been, inarguably, a sustained backlash against the social justice movements of the last decade—one that might have damaged cherished causes of the left. Black Lives Matter morphed into Defund the Police, which burned brightly before petering out. Police reform is not discussed nearly as much as it once was; small-bore reforms have come to departments around the country and progressive prosecutors were elected, but the sweeping change sought by the activist class has yet to materialize. Some of these prosecutors, in subsequent elections, have been driven from office, and a Democratic governor in New York, Kathy Hochul, has steadily chipped away at the bail reform laws passed in 2019. Another high-profile police killing could revive Black Lives Matter, but it's a frail movement that needs tragedy to galvanize voters. It's also no longer clear even that will be enough: the brutal 2024 police killing of a New York City teenager named Win Rozario, captured on film, did not trigger any mass protests. Liberals, sadly, mostly ignored the family.

The immigrant rights movement, #MeToo, and Covid hawkishness engendered a similar blowback. All were well-intentioned. Donald Trump's open hostility to immigrants spurred the rights movement on, bringing new scrutiny to Immigration and Customs Enforcement and the policy of child separation. Democrat-run cities proudly declared themselves sanctuaries that wouldn't cooperate with federal law enforcement. Support for open borders, or something close, surged, and the *Times*' Nicholas Kristof would come to call Trump's immigration policies "evil." By 2024, the rapid increase in migrants crossing the border led President Joe Biden to aggressively restrict their entry and Kristof to declare that America must "settle for accepting a fraction of those eager to come, and determining that fraction is the political question before us, with many trade-offs to consider."

Kristof, something of a liberal weathervane, captured the new sentiment, with few Democrats championing immigration like they had in the Trump years. The Abolish ICE movement was long gone—even Alexandria Ocasio-Cortez, one of its early champions, didn't mention it anymore. #MeToo hasn't quite faded in the same way. For good reason, there has been far more attention paid to workplace harassment in the 2020s than there was before the movement rose to prominence in 2017. There will never again be someone like Harvey Weinstein who harasses and assaults women, for decades, with impunity. Overreach, though, sapped momentum for the cause. Kirsten Gillibrand forced Al Franken out of the Senate, only to make Franken something of a liberal martyr and Gillibrand herself a damaged political entity. When she ran for president in 2019, she attracted little support, and her profile in the Senate shrunk. The darker turn of the #MeToo backlash manifested in the rise of misogynistic celebrities like Andrew Tate and the birth of reactionary online spaces for men. The movement, overall, wasn't helped by the crumbling of the Women's March. There simply weren't any prominent leaders, free of scandal, to push the cause forward in the 2020s.

And what of Trust the Science? We can now think honestly about what happened in the early years of the pandemic. Covid was devastating for the nation and world, and leaders everywhere scrambled to react to such an unprecedented, deadly threat. After initially decrying the use of face masks and even Covid alarmism itself, liberals rapidly evolved into Covid hawks once it became clear Trump was going to downplay the virus as much as possible. (It must be remembered that in early 2020 it was considered right-coded to care too much about coronavirus because it was coming from China and Silicon Valley types seemed most troubled.) Early shutdowns were very much necessary and leaders in California and Washington State saved lives through fast action. New York politicians dithered and the city suffered for it. Covid policy, though, became far less straightforward in the latter half of 2020 and into 2021. Liberal Covid hawks insisted on prolonged school closures that proved deleterious and likely harmed any future lockdown efforts if another pandemic does arise. Vaccine policy was confounding enough that the anti-vax movement grew far stronger than it was before the pandemic, with the virulently anti-vax Robert F. Kennedy Jr. emerging, for a time, as a prominent third-party presidential candidate. (After Trump won, Kennedy became the new Health and Human Services Secretary.) Public health officials promised the new vaccines could stop the spread of Covid completely, and they helped craft policy designed around this premise—limiting bars, restaurants, and other indoor spaces to the vaccinated, and taking the radical step of binding employment to vaccination status. Once it became clear the new Covid vaccines could *not* stop the spread of the virus—they helped prevent serious illness but people were still getting infected, regardless of their boosters—the policies that public health officials and Democratic politicians defended no longer made much sense. To make matters worse, rare side effects of the vaccines were greatly downplayed on the left, allowing, in turn, anti-vax misinformation to flourish further, as it became verboten to ask any questions about the vaccines.

In 2024, the *New York Times* acknowledged, for the first time at length, those who were suffering from side effects of the Covid vaccines. None of this, really, should have been a surprise: unlike most other vaccines, which are studied and tested for many years before heading to market, the Pfizer, Moderna, and Johnson & Johnson vaccines were developed and distributed over the course of a single year. The point here is not to relitigate the Covid wars. It's simply to suggest that it all could have been different had the politics not been so rigid. More honesty and less absolutism from public health officials would have gone a long way. Vaccine passports fueled conspiracy theories. Public health liberals in the United States today are in a far worse position than they were at the start of the decade. Skepticism of Covid vaccines has bled over into a wider distrust for all vaccines, even those that have clearly worked for more than a half century. Measles reemerged.

All of this—the decline of Black Lives Matter, the slippage of #MeToo, the end of the Trust the Science era—pointed to a left in retreat. On the electoral front, it was becoming harder for progressives to unseat moderate incumbents. But amid these struggles was another reality that few in America could ignore if they were paying close enough attention—austerity politics was a dying politics. And it was dying, in part, because the left had been able to revive itself so dramatically in the 2010s. Without Occupy Wall Street and the Bernie Sanders 2016 campaign, there was no renewed focus on economic issues and income inequality. There was no shifting of the terms of debate. It might have been simplistic to argue that a losing presidential campaign and an amorphous protest movement dealt a blow to neoliberalism, but it all mattered in the sense that the modern centrist Democrats now looked very different than those who had campaigned two or three decades earlier. The Blue

Dog Democrats of the 2020s did not stump on shrinking welfare, cutting corporate taxes, and boosting free trade. On their website they wrote vaguely about "fiscal responsibility" and the deficit, but they offered no specific federal budget cuts—no social safety net or anti-poverty programs to target. Most of them, especially in the House, did not triangulate; a vast majority voted for Biden's far-reaching infrastructure and climate change legislation, which was impacted directly by progressives. On trade, they were all largely protectionist and anti-China. They were skeptical of Big Tech. Endangered swing-district Democrats like Marie Gluesenkamp Perez maintained a populist sheen. Her top campaign issues, for example, were rejecting corporate PAC money, safeguarding abortion rights, and combating inflation. But unlike some economists and pundits on both the right and center-left who might contend that slashing federal spending and reducing demand are needed to bring down prices, Gluesenkamp Perez wanted to raise the minimum wage and stop corporate "price gouging."

This, in its own way, was remarkable. If austerity politics was going to make a comeback, it would be in the mid-2020s, with enough prominent voices blaming the major stimulus spending passed during the Trump and Biden administrations for the inflation of that period. Centrist pundits had been pining for the old Simpson-Bowles commission, established under President Barack Obama to aggressively reduce the deficit. The commission argued for tax hikes to be paired with cuts to Social

Security and Medicare. In that same period, Obama partnered with Congress to initiate the sequester: mandatory cuts to domestic spending and defense. These policies, popular with both parties at the time, proved to be both strategically and economically harmful. The post-crash economy was under-stimulated and required more deficit spending to boost employment and growth. In the late 2000s and early 2010s, jobs were scarce, wages were low, the housing market had collapsed, and local governments were laying off employees in droves. The stimulus Obama was able to pass in the Democrat-controlled Congress helped the United States avoid a second depression, but it was not nearly large enough to combat an economic malaise that would last nearly a decade and boost the fortunes of a populist Republican outsider who decided to seek the nomination in 2016.

It was Trump, as much as Sanders or Occupy, who doomed austerity politics. The right-wing populists of the early 2010s were the Tea Party politicians who sought radical reductions in taxes and government spending. They railed against the stimulus, the Affordable Care Act, and any expansion of the social safety net. They cheered on the gutting of local governments. Their stars included Ted Cruz, Michele Bachmann, Tim Scott, and Jim DeMint. Paul Ryan, a charismatic deficit hawk, was their intellectual architect, and funding was pumped in by the Koch Brothers and Dick Armey. What characterized the Tea Party, as much as its bitter antipathy for the first Black president, was a savage fiscal conservatism. If the culture of the Tea Party remained in the GOP—the toppling of Kevin McCarthy was, in every way, a page ripped from the Tea Party's playbook—the lust for budget-cutting, until Elon Musk's DOGE, mostly vanished. Trump himself, in 2016, campaigned as a skeptic of free trade and large corporations, and promised, unlike his rivals, to not slash Social Security and Medicare. He proved the Republican base didn't care much for supply-side economics or the ideology of Milton Friedman. It wanted culture war, which the incendiary Trump could do better than any Republican alive. The Tea Party successors, like Marjorie Taylor Greene, cared far more about flaying liberal pieties, denouncing immigrants, and indulging in peculiar conspiracy theories than about shrinking anti-poverty programs and healthcare. Once Trump and the Ryan-led House failed to repeal the Affordable Care Act, the issue disappeared almost entirely from the stump. Few talked about trickle-down or Reaganomics anymore. For most Republicans, Trump had supplanted Ronald Reagan in the pantheon anyway.

This did not mean Trump was a genuine economic populist. As president, he oversaw a sweeping corporate tax cut, and he was much friendlier toward megacorporations when he ran in 2024. He courted and won large, dissident segments of Silicon Valley, including Elon Musk and his fellow billionaire David Sacks, and converted the Winklevoss twins, who had co-founded

Facebook, into supporters after embracing cryptocurrency. He was a threat to the tangible populist accomplishments of the Biden administration. Biden's appointees revived antitrust and took a much more skeptical approach to how banks and corporations treated consumers. One bright spot, for the anti-monopoly set, was Trump's choice of J. D. Vance as a running mate. Vance had offered praise for Lina Khan, Biden's chair of the Federal Trade Commission, and he seemed to be an earnest skeptic of monopoly power. There were sections of his convention speech that sounded like they could have been cribbed from Bernie Sanders or Sherrod Brown, the progressive Democratic senator from Ohio.

Austerity, then, was withering. No Democratic faction was calling for it and the Republicans seemed to care about other things. Inflation had not buoyed the deficit hawks or the supply-side champions, possibly because many politicians and voters remembered how frail the post-2008 economy was and how unpopular austerity had proved to be. The right-wing populists in America and Europe had, in a similar fashion, chosen culture over economics, and politicians in both continents remembered how aggressive budget cuts scarred a generation of working- and middle-class families. European austerity was even more severe than the American variety, and weighed heavily on the legacy of the German-centric European Union. In the United States, it was possible inflation had not spurred an austerity revival because there was a growing recognition that price increases were a global phenomenon. If austerity remained buried, far away from Democratic and Republican platforms, this represented one of the great undersold victories of the economic left. After decades in the wilderness—from the Carter-era neoliberalism to Reagan's attacks on the New Deal to Bill Clinton's Third Way—the left could lay claim to a future that didn't promise the retreat of government from everyday life.

It might have been a single day, in the fall of 2011, that heralded the future of the American left. John Lewis, the congressman and civil rights icon, arrived at Woodruff Park in downtown Atlanta, hoping to address a burgeoning crowd. He was there, that October afternoon, to lend solidarity to Atlanta's Occupy encampment. The Occupy movement, catalyzing a fresh and crackling rage over income inequality, had leaped from Manhattan to the rest of America. Lewis was proud, even excited, and had a simple message for the protesters: I stand with you, I support you.

He hadn't asked beforehand to speak at the encampment, but in situations like these, when a famed politician arrives at the site of a fledgling protest, the reaction is usually straightforward. He is cheered, or at least beckoned forward.

But Lewis's appearance had not been scheduled. A debate erupted at the general assembly over whether he could interrupt their current agenda, which hadn't allotted time for Lewis or any other public figure. Ultimately, the congressman was blocked from speaking and asked to return another time. Publicly at least, he did not take offense. "It's OK," Lewis said. "They didn't deny me."

Still, an internet firestorm raged, with critiques of Occupy breaking along racial lines. Lewis, a Black man, was said to have been disrespected, at least temporarily, by privileged white protesters, even if the reality was more complex. Later on, broader ruminations would come on the nature of Occupy, which both seized imaginations and drew condemnation for its lack of coherent policy demands. Noted, too, was the fraught, consensus-driven decision-making model of the encampments, where horizontal democracy was so prized that even sympathetic politicians of great renown could not intrude.

The leaderless left was born. Then marginal, and initially written off, it would never vanish entirely, serving as something of a static undercurrent to left organizing everywhere. But what is a leaderless left, exactly? One challenge was that almost no one would identify with the term. Another was its sheer amorphousness. Broadly defined, though, the leaderless left had a deep and lasting suspicion of leaders and personalities. Out of ambition or even fear—digital surveillance, online harassment, and the rise of doxxing had all dramatically raised the price of public engagement—this flank of the left did not seek to anoint famed activists or politicians to lead them.

There was an overriding feeling among younger voters that those in power, Democrats and Republicans alike, were inexorably disconnected from their struggles. It was an age, for them, without heroes.

If there was a moment when the era of the leaderless left first announced itself—when the suspicions of hierarchy and personality were manifested most plain—it might have been that day when Lewis ambled up to Occupy Atlanta. After lying dormant in the personality-first 2010s, that spirit is now everywhere, resentments festering at all those—whether celebrities, politicians, or so-called professional activists—who fronted, or successfully co-opted, past movements. It was also evident in Black Lives Matter and the subsequent push to defund the police, which briefly elevated certain activists and academics, like the anti-racism scholar Ibram X. Kendi, but never coalesced around any particular personality for very long. When Bernie Sanders was campaigning for the presidency, the leaderless had a leader, but there was no great public yearning for what might come after the octogenarian Vermont senator exited the scene. Meanwhile, the outcome of the 2020 Democratic primary amounted to the greatest of all comedowns for a certain generation of young progressives who had believed, for a fleeting time, that America's destiny was intertwined with their own. Instead of the democratic socialist Sanders, it was Biden, the very embodiment of establishment moderation, who captured the nomination. As president, Biden governed, on economic matters, to the left of his immediate predecessors, but this didn't change the fact that he was decidedly not Sanders and still remained deferential to the institutions and interest groups that the Vermont senator was willing to rage against.

All of this came to the fore after the October 7 attacks, when Hamas took hostages and killed more than 1,100 Israeli civilians, and the Israeli government retaliated by waging a war that drove the Gazan death toll into the tens of thousands. Biden's inability to stem the carnage alienated young voters who took an increasingly dim view of Israel; for many left activists and organizations, the plight of the Palestinians was the overriding concern. Palestinian activists themselves tagged Biden "Genocide Joe," arguing there was little difference between his victory and Trump's. One told me it was a brutal choice between genocide and fascism.

The individual had melted away—more so, even, than in Occupy, Black Lives Matter, #MeToo, or any other leftist upsurge of the last decade. It was not the Squad—nor Sanders, certainly—who stood at the vanguard of the exploding, multifarious, and unabashedly radical pro-Palestinian movement, what I've termed the Palestine Left. The Palestinian American representative Rashida Tlaib, too press-shy, was arguably ancillary to what was happening, and even Ocasio-Cortez was targeted by activists for her initial reluctance to deem Israel's war in Gaza a genocide. Occupy, for all its hostility to political personalities, nonetheless helped to mint several, including a Harvard bankruptcy professor seeking a Senate seat in Massachusetts.

"I created much of the intellectual foundation for what they do," Elizabeth Warren proudly proclaimed in 2011. The civil rights era, of course, produced numerous famed leaders and personalities. Beyond Martin Luther King Jr. and Malcolm X, there was Rosa Parks, Bayard Rustin, and Ralph Abernathy. Black Panthers like Bobby Seale were household names. Students for a Democratic Society, which radicalized and eventually crumbled from infighting, elevated Tom Hayden; the Free Speech movement minted Mario Savio; and the counterculture kicked up its own offbeat celebrities, like Jerry Rubin and Abbie Hoffman. The feminist movement boasted numerous headliners, including Betty Friedan, Germaine Greer, and Bella Abzug, the pioneering congresswoman. Out of that same era came Michael Harrington, the well-known author and political theorist who, as the left retreated, founded the Democratic Socialists of America (DSA) in 1982.

"The twentieth century left always had someone who embodied the movement," Maurice Isserman, a professor of history at Hamilton College, told me. "In the past, you could say, 'I'm a Michael Harrington socialist' and that meant something, or 'I'm, you know, a Eugene Debs socialist.' It gave you a political identity. It was a shorthand for the whole idea. You don't have to hand somebody *Das Kapital* to explain your position if you've got Eugene Debs out there."

Those within the Palestinian movement believed the fear of doxxing prevented activists from stepping forward and becoming known. Formidable Israel supporters like the billionaire Bill Ackman made dogged and raging efforts to publicly identify protesters, especially at colleges, in a bid to blacklist them from future employment. Others have argued that there is a danger to investing too much political capital in any individual, since they all can be fallible. The anti-Trump Women's March eventually devolved into scandal, with allegations of antisemitism lodged against its star organizers.

In the 1960s and '70s, even as notions of participatory democracy and bottom-up organizing were being championed, leading activists were far more enthusiastic about parading through the media's glare—and the media itself was "more committed to the idea of political celebrity, trying to identify and promote people as leading voices," according to Jeremy Varon, a historian at the New School who has studied postwar American social movements. "There's a kind of paucity of public figures now who lend their name and reputation to a cause. Leadership is intrinsically bad, hierarchy is bad, and everyone loves viral, self-reproducing protest."

We may be sliding into a new age, one of "personality exhaustion," in the words of the culture writer Mo Diggs. Parasocial bonds with individuals, particularly online, defined much of the 2010s—whether in politics or on YouTube or Twitter. It was boom time for megalithic influencers. Some conservatives and pro-Israel commentators blame TikTok for fomenting anti-Zionism on its platform, but the real upheaval the social media giant triggered was its "For You" page, which placed emphasis on short videos and memes over memorable individuals. Twitter itself, rebranded X by Elon Musk, lost its purchase as the preeminent news-breaking hub; blue checks were now for sale, unreliable information clogged up the feeds, and actual news articles were suppressed by Musk's algorithm in favor of video and images uploaded directly to X.

It was this vacuum that TikTok filled, especially TikTok Live, where brutal images from Gaza can stream night and day, unmediated. As another culture writer, Kyle Raymond Fitzpatrick, observed in 2023, TikTok has increasingly become a platform of ideas and images, rather than individuals or personalities. There are "stars" but they're not like those of yesteryear—or even their 2010s forerunners. The food items, pranks, and kitschy dances are the point, not the quasi-celebrities performing them. In the wake of Israel's war in Gaza, TikTok became, more than ever, an images and ideas medium, conversation around rocket attacks and genocide supplanting the people advancing the arguments. If individuals were featured, they were the victims themselves in Gaza. In the new era, it matters less who in particular produces the soaring rhetoric, with speechifying itself—once so fame-making in the 1960s—growing mostly irrelevant.

Meanwhile, politicians and influencers with left sympathies were unable or unwilling to keep up, to rise again, as they might have for prior social justice movements, to the crest of the new wave. The Jenner/Kardashian clan, for one, agonized over how high to go. A pro-Palestinian activist—or someone furiously anti-Israel, hoping for the Jewish State's dissolution—simply couldn't find many celebrities, politicians, or famed activists speaking just like them. All of this was in stark contrast to the George Floyd protests of 2020, when celebrities and corporate behemoths could comfortably release Black Lives Matter statements and promise new diversity initiatives. The NBA painted "Black Lives Matter" on its hardcourts, and the NFL, perhaps the most culturally conservative of the major North American sports leagues, did the same in its end zones.

Powerful political donors could stomach Black Lives Matter. There was no equivalent of the American Israel Public Affairs Committee spending millions opposing it. When the New York congressman Jamaal Bowman, a champion of social justice movements and defunding the police, won a shock primary in 2020, he immediately aligned with AOC.

As outlined in Chapter 1, the American Israel Public Affairs Committee (AIPAC) and affiliated organizations unleashed more than $14 million against Bowman, and in 2024 he lost handily to a primary challenger, George Latimer. Bowman's own political missteps, unrelated to Israel, also played a role in his downfall. Regardless, a willing public leader for the Palestine Left—more unabashed in his foreign policy views than Ocasio-Cortez—was no more.

No others, it seems, are on the horizon.

For the pro-Palestinian youth, distrust in all mainstream institutions and personalities was inordinately high. Their faith in the political system and the mainstream media was so minimal that there was little interest in hunting out designated tribunes—why bother having spokespeople to talk to those who despise us? There were no individuals they could look to, perhaps, other than themselves. Certainly, none that, like Students for Justice in Palestine, were going to openly celebrate the Hamas attacks as a "unity Intifada" requiring "confrontation by any means necessary." (Other anti-Zionist organizations, like Jewish Voice for Peace, strongly condemned the violence of October 7.)

The Palestine Left didn't view Harris much differently. She was unlikely, for example, to accede to Tlaib's demand for a permanent ceasefire and an end to American military aid to Israel. She would never go further and embrace a binational state, one that Israelis and Palestinians share without a mandated Jewish majority.

As much as her Arab American constituents might have soured on Biden and Harris, Tlaib was still unwilling to campaign for the presidency. When frustrations boiled over so dramatically that the Palestine Left decided to challenge Biden, there was no candidate to run. On one hand, there was an obvious enough reason why: the war in Gaza had begun only a few months before primary season, too little time for a contender to raise significant amounts of cash, assemble a viable campaign, and begin competitively stumping in large, expensive states. But a placeholder—an activist in possession of visible clout or native charisma—could have emerged. None did. Instead, a new movement was born, urging voters to choose "uncommitted" on their ballots or, in the case of states like New York, leave them blank altogether. Organizers touted it as a success, pointing to the roughly thirty delegates won, but it was notable that, unlike in 2016 and 2020, there was no challenger, no actual individual to carry the cause forward. Sanders had already endorsed Biden. No one, it seemed, wanted to risk angering the Democratic establishment, even over the fate of the Palestinians. The primary season came and went.

These delegates represented less than 1 percent of those who attended the 2024 convention in Chicago. In 2016, Sanders had brought nearly 2,000 delegates, nearly half the total that would nominate Hillary Clinton.

Activists on the Palestine Left weren't concerned. "The fact that people were voting for an idea and not an inherently flawed individual as any candidate contributed to how we had such a strong showing in Michigan," Abbas Aliwieh, a leader of the Uncommitted national movement, told me. "That's one of the real sources of power of this movement: we convinced people to vote for the idea that our Democratic Party should be anti-war."

The more moderate and center-left Democrats

confronted their own crisis in the wake of Biden's disastrous June TV debate that put him further behind Trump in the polls. He held on until he couldn't any longer: on July 21, facing a revolt within the party, he announced he would not run again and quickly endorsed Harris. *Unity* was the word on every liberal's lips, as well as *relief*. Harris carried her own drawbacks into the presidential race—her prior campaign had ended terribly and her electoral track record in California was middling—but she was, at age fifty-nine, plainly equipped to aggressively prosecute the case against Trump. She could speak, with vigor, on safeguarding abortion rights. Ocasio-Cortez, who had remained at Biden's side when party moderates were openly breaking from him, swiftly supported her.

What Harris's rapid ascension masked, for the moment at least, was a fascinating—and rather new—fissure between those who had rooted their Weltanschauungs, almost exclusively, in Israel and Gaza and those on the left who did not talk about Palestine at all. This second faction, which I've called the Blue Liberals, was still dominant on cable television, on social media, and in prestige media outlets. They were embodied in Democratic Party–aligned pundits like Jen Psaki, Ron Filipkowski, Aaron Rupar, and Majid Padellan, who ran the BrooklynDad_Defiant! social media account, which boasted more than 1 million followers. Blue Liberals had been fully committed to boosting Biden and flipped easily to Harris; blasting away at Trump, they framed the presidential election as wholly existential, a choice between democracy and fascism.

Unlike the Palestine Left, Blue Liberals tended to be personality-obsessed. They had a pantheon of quondam idols. There was Robert Mueller, the Republican former FBI director who probed Russian interference into the 2016 election. There were intense love affairs with James Comey and Michael Avenatti, the former Stormy Daniels lawyer who ended up in prison on extortion and embezzlement convictions. The Vindman brothers, high-ranking army veterans who publicly opposed Trump, remained in good standing. Eugene Vindman won the Democratic nomination for a congressional seat in Virginia.

Blue Liberals and Palestine Leftists raged in parallel universes. Occasionally, there were breaches, or figures who moved between the two factions, like Pod Save America host Tommy Vietor, who reviled Trump but also angrily denounced the Netanyahu government and joined some Obama alums, including Benjamin Rhodes, in criticizing Biden's foreign policy. Most Blue Liberals, though, were focused on Trump's trials, Samuel Alito's flag controversies, and Harris's election odds. If, in the telling of some pro-Palestinian activists, the presidential election meant little as Gazan civilians were being slaughtered, with a Trump victory only a marginally worse outcome, Blue Liberals chose to see 2024 as one of the great pivot points in American history. The two sides did not argue so much as talk past each other, to audiences that might never tangle.

Democrats focused squarely on the fall elections held a disdain for the Palestine Left—if they thought of them at all. Others believed they were too marginal, despite their popularity with the youth. And those Blue Liberals who didn't dismiss the impact of the Palestine Left viewed them as being more destructive than feckless, like the radicals of the late '60s willing to torpedo Humphrey even if it meant Nixon was elected president.

Among mainstream Democrats, it was the Blue Liberals who, for now, won out. And as Sanders receded—and Ocasio-Cortez, in her mid-thirties, gradually gained seniority—political existence grew more perilous for a left that eschewed defined leadership and had become too comfortable with street protest. It was true that the left organizations themselves, like DSA, the Working Families Party, and Justice Democrats, which first helped boost Ocasio-Cortez, were enduring and still winning downballot elections. It was also true that they played no role in Biden's departure or Harris's rise, and had a limited impact on her selection of a running mate.

What did Harris owe the left—either those affiliated with Sanders or the leaderless crying out for peace in Gaza? Obama alums more tolerant of corporate power, like David Plouffe and Eric Holder, gravitated immediately to the Harris campaign. Well-heeled donors were suddenly thrilled for what was to come. On foreign policy, the Uncommitted movement carried too few delegates to win any meaningful floor flights, since no individual candidate had accumulated enough votes to hold sway at a convention. The rest of the protesters were confined to the streets of Chicago, far away from the coronation of Harris.

Biden's debate failures initially proved damaging to the immediate futures of both factions. Blue Liberals had an incumbent who was viewed, by wide swaths of the electorate, as too elderly and inept to govern—and fresh evidence emerged that he was a drag on the House and Senate candidates who were outpolling him. The Palestine Left, meanwhile, could not position itself to take advantage of the failure of the standard-bearer they had opposed for so many months. They were bystanders, and little more. Sanders was out stumping for Biden, traveling across America to urge his base to give the president one more chance. When I asked Sanders, upon his arrival in New York to support the doomed Jamaal Bowman candidacy, if he had any opinions on the burgeoning Israel skepticism on the left—the growing number of young people who now endorse a single state for Jews and Palestinians, without an explicit Jewish majority—Sanders didn't want to engage at all. "It's not an issue I hear a whole lot. What I hear, overwhelmingly, with maybe very, very few exceptions, is that Hamas is a terrorist organization pledged to destroy Israel and committed an atrocious war crime on October 7. That's what I hear." He added that "Netanyahu's right-wing, racist, extremist government has gone to war against the Palestinian people."

What was more difficult to influence, absent any genuine kingmakers, was ideology and message discipline. There were few who could adjudicate, in the public arena, on whether "From the River to the Sea" was a call for the peaceful liberation of the Palestinian people or for the eradication of Jews in Israel. There was no one well-positioned enough to insist that the small number of leftists who demanded sympathy for or even solidarity with Hamas didn't, in fact, speak for the broader movement. And Sanders, absent a single disciple, could not guarantee his issues would outlast him, particularly Medicare for All, which was never seriously entertained when Democrats controlled both chambers of Congress in 2021 and 2022. In the Senate, Harris had co-sponsored Sanders's sweeping healthcare legislation but then disavowed it on the campaign trail. Universal healthcare, once a lodestar issue for the progressive left, faded from view. The energy around the Harris campaign against Trump, with the war in Gaza as a continual backdrop, overshadowed any greater worries about the leaderlessness of the new left. Mass protest, and the activist energy that coursed through the pro-Palestinian college encampments, seemed to suffice. Some progressives fretted over finding another Sanders or someone more potent—an avowed leftist who might seize the Democratic nomination and win like Biden and Obama did—while others preferred to focus on the present: the season of protest, and the Sanders acolytes who did hold office. Protest itself, so easily staged and replicated, could be intoxicating.

Horizontalism, as Occupy and Black Lives Matters showed, only gets a movement so far. Enduring organizations with defined, well-regarded leaders fronting them are needed for nudging America closer to the social democracy progressives long for—or, in the case of the pro-Palestinian movement, a foreign policy that somehow reverses the occupation of the West Bank, rebuilds Gaza, and establishes a nation for the Palestinians. Much of this will be decided in the years ahead, as the left transmogrifies beyond Sanders's shadow, and street protests, as they always do, ebb. If leaders are unwanted today, they may not be rejected tomorrow; volatility, if nothing else, will remain the defining feature of our political age.

5

Israel

My late father, a Jew who once lived on a kibbutz in the early 1960s, would always speak of Israel with sadness and resignation. He was of a cohort that no longer exists, the socialist Zionist, and over time he retained the former identification without any of the latter. With one of his rueful smiles, he would say to me that Israel, in retrospect, had been a mistake. He was an atheist, so the relations this patch of sand had with the Torah meant little to him. He identified, far more, with the Zionists of the early twentieth century who were open to many different outcomes for a Jewish homeland. British East Africa, Dutch Suriname, and the Argentine were all, at one time, debated as possibilities. During the First World War, the British Empire announced support for an eventual Jewish homeland in Palestine. The Holocaust would accelerate those preparations. By 1948, after a ferocious war and the expulsion of the Arabs, the State of Israel was established. My father's view, in subsequent decades, was that the Europeans should have been forced to carve out a nation for the Jews locally. Most of them knew Europe, not Palestine, as their homeland, and wouldn't it be nice to have the Jews in Alsace-Lorraine? But the antisemites of Europe were not about to cede land to these desperate refugees. Let them ride to the desert and sort it out themselves.

As an American and a Jew descended from Eastern Europe, I have always had an uneasy relationship with Israel. Again and again, people like me have been forced to answer for a nation that we are not bound to in any meaningful way; I have never visited Israel and I'm not sure I ever will. To ask an American Jew to account for Israel is not so different than demanding an answer from them for the ongoing crisis in Sudan. No apoplectic left- or right-wing mobs are demanding politicians, celebrities, pundits, or minor cultural figures formulate opinions on the Tigray war or an invasion of Armenia. But what you think about Israel and the Palestinians—or Palestine, if you want to appear particularly progressive—defines entirely what you are and what you will be in the political arena.

It is all a catastrophe, a cataclysm. There are no other words. Hamas, a political organization that has had a stranglehold on the blockaded Gaza Strip since I graduated high school, launched a terrorist attack that slaughtered more than a thousand Israeli civilians. There was no justification for the massacre. The families and children living on the border with Gaza were not posing any threat to the oppressed Palestinians. They died solely for Hamas to make a political statement, one it paid dearly for. Or rather, one that the people of Gaza, terrified and destitute, are paying for. Hamas will probably make out fine in all of this. They knew exactly what they were doing.

Israel is a contradiction. At some point, you can no longer be an ethnostate and a democracy. At some point, you will not govern with any reason or compassion when only one political ideology dominates the body politic. Like George W. Bush after 9/11, Benjamin Netanyahu was bathed in the glow of a new holy war, one that would slaughter many more civilians on the other side. Like Bush, perhaps, Netanyahu will belatedly come in for his own reckoning—the Hamas attack, like 9/11, represents an enormous security and intelligence failure—and his government will eventually be brought down. But the *liberal* Zionists, the many Democrats in America who now so cheerfully wave Israeli flags, must understand that there is no hope. Their kind, in Israel, are extinguished. Bibi marches to the drum of the far right and serves at *their* pleasure. When he loses power or dies, there will be no Golda Meir presiding over this land of the Jews. It will be the muscular Jews, ultrareligious and bloodthirsty, who will get all that they want. Gaza will be flattened. How many of the 2 million can be displaced or outright killed? This is the new war.

Two-state solution, one-state solution, no solution. Israel possesses, thanks to the United States, one of the world's great militaries. There is no overthrowing Israel. The sort of Zionists who argued it was in the best interests of Israel to hand the Palestinians their own nation—allowing the moderating forces of democracy to build, over time, a relationship between the two countries—are long gone, either driven out of public life or dead. The most idealistic solution, the one most popular with American leftists, is the single, multinational state, a democracy where everyone has an equal vote, an equal say. This, in a just world, would be the outcome, but it will not happen. Not now, not tomorrow, not ever. A multinational state is not a *Jewish* state, just as it's not written into the Constitution that America is for the white Protestants and no one else. The Jews might get outvoted, just like two Catholics and even a Black man became president here. Bibi and his allies won't allow that to happen. Nor will the United States. The bombardment of Gaza makes that clear.

Americans don't quite comprehend the depravity of it all, the nullity. We are used to answers. Pull this lever, propose this policy, fund this initiative, punish these people. It will all work itself out! Those who call the Palestinian situation apartheid are correct, but what of it? What now? Has BDS *changed* anything? The anti-Zionist Jews must comprehend, too, that the Palestinians will only credit them so much for their solidarity. The Israel hawks, ludicrously calcified, can't fathom Palestinian humanity. To them, all hatred of Israel is antisemitic. The people who hate the Jews hate Israel. But there are plenty people who revile what the Israeli government, the greater power by titanic magnitudes, does. How it punishes, how it kills—how it strangles the Palestinians and expects quietude, somehow, out of

Gaza. The United States could have forced a ceasefire, demanded Israel stand down. The bombs already dropped should have been enough. This is all the liberals, so neutered otherwise, can hope for—that the death toll satiates Netanyahu.

"I am a patriot—of the Fourteenth Ward, Brooklyn, where I was raised. The rest of the United States doesn't exist for me, except as idea, or history, or literature." Henry Miller's words in *Black Spring* have moved through me since I was nineteen. Best known for his surrealistic and sexualized romps through Paris, Miller wrote tenderly on his first years in Williamsburg, when he ran wild through its gloriously fetid streets, love and violence on the offering in equal measure. For Miller, Williamsburg was his homeland; he could write with venom about America but never his neighborhood. There was no contradiction here. His patriotism was reserved for Driggs Avenue. The rest of it was an abstraction, nothing that could touch the heart.

That sentiment is familiar. I came of age on the other end of Brooklyn a century later, in an enclave that was slowly shedding its immigrant and working-class character. Bay Ridge could be a world unto itself, nestled in the shadow of an enormous suspension bridge and ribboned by highways, fog-swept and wind-bitten and gorgeous. I grew up surrounded by Irish, Italians, and the occasional Arab. As a New York Jew, I was in a distinct minority, and this could be a strange place for someone like me to be. Stroll through Park Slope, the

Upper West Side, or Midwood and you will be confronted by every flavor of Jew—God-fearing, godless, socialist, right-wing, shomer Shabbat, secular, Hasidic—and come to believe, wrongly, that this is what America is—a place where the Jew and Christian exist at parity. Until college, I didn't know there were towns on Long Island that are entirely Jewish, not just Orthodox but culturally that way, children already primed for their inevitable Birthright trips. Bay Ridge has a single Jewish temple, and I went there for Hebrew school lessons on Sundays, indifferent except for story and snack time, when I chewed on animal crackers and thought vaguely about how all the animals fit on Noah's Ark. The Morah didn't like me when I asked about the asteroids and the dinosaurs, and why there weren't dinosaurs in the Torah. My bar mitzvah was held in Bergen Beach, not Bay Ridge, because the temple there had a larger ballroom and it was a two-for-one kind of deal. I learned how to read my Torah passages from a portly cantor who spoke in a thick Hebrew accent and once made me cry because I hadn't studied hard enough. Once the bar mitzvah ended, my knowledge of Judaism dribbled slowly out of me. There were batting averages and anime sagas to absorb. My religion would make no more demands of me.

The glory and tragedy of Israel was supposed to matter to me, but never did. It didn't matter for a reason so obvious that other Jews kept missing it, as if so blinded by the sun's golden light they forgot what it was that was burning their eyes in the first place. I was born in New York City. I am an American citizen. I have no family in Israel and no descendants from there. I am an Ashkenazi Jew, with great-grandparents who migrated out of Eastern Europe during various waves of antisemitic violence in the nineteenth century. These were the Russians, the Belarussians, the Pale of Settlement Jews, the backbone of America's first socialist wave. They streamed through Manhattan, Brooklyn, and the Bronx, remaking the new century there. They were the tailors, the garment workers, the candy store owners, the scholars, and the gangsters. Their children and grandchildren wrote best-selling novels. Some went into politics. My great-grandfather opened a gas station to give his developmentally disabled son something to do with his days—while his son tinkered with automobiles, he read Tolstoy in Russian and smoked his pipe. These Jews could only be so entranced by Zion, a theoretical country somewhere in the world only for them. What was Zion against Orchard Street, the Grand Concourse, Ocean Avenue? They had already left one country to come to this one. The United States may have been Christian in character, but it was not Christian by law; this distinction mattered, and it gave Jews the escape hatch out of the shtetls that they needed.

I understand, intellectually, why it is I'm supposed to care for Israel—Zion was promised at the end of one world war and guaranteed after the Holocaust—and why it matters, now, that Israel was attacked. I grieve for the civilians Hamas slaughtered. But I grieve, too, for civilians slaughtered everywhere, and I struggle to care more about one foreign country over another. Well, the Zionist has an easy retort: *you are Jewish*. But I, as an American Jew, never demanded an ethnostate. I have never been to Israel and would not feel safer there than I would in Bay Ridge, Brooklyn. I have never been the victim of an antisemitic attack here. I do not wear a kippah, and never will. Perhaps the frum prefer Israel. But in their private moments I doubt they'd say they're better off in Israel than they would be in Borough Park or Midwood or Rockland County.

Zionism might be of service to the Israeli Jew—compelled into the military, hungry for a region-immolating war—but it does little for the American Jew, happily moored here. It actively punishes, even endangers. An entire religion must answer, in one form or another, for the actions of a particular nation-state. We must account for a government that we never elected and never will. The Knesset isn't the New York State Legislature or Congress. Benjamin Netanyahu doesn't live in the White House. It was an annoyance to be an American traveling abroad and have to answer for President Trump, but at least there was a logic baked into such casual idiocy. The most ardent Zionists must reckon with how much their advocacy has been a gift to antisemites. European antisemites, in the last century, fantasized about packing up all the Jews in Germany and France and England and depositing them in the desert.

To Palestine, with all of you! The cynical antisemite, a hundred years later, can corral a New York Jew on the street and berate him for the sins of Netanyahu. Do you see what your religion has done? You've blockaded 2 million people. You've killed tens of thousands in Gaza, far exceeding the number of dead Hamas claimed in Israel, far exceeding the number of hostages taken. You are the colonizers, the oppressors—you, the Jew!

What does the Jew say back? The Zionist is giddy to conflate Judaism with Netanyahu, Benny Gantz, and the IDF. Temple Shalom in Bergen Beach, Brooklyn, is supposed to have everything to do with the occupied West Bank. The convergence of antisemitism and Zionism is too unsettling for most American Jews to contemplate for more than a few black seconds. The insect brain clicks back in—support Israel, support Jews—and the consequences can never be mulled, not really, not when the beast looms in full view. The anti-Zionists, of course, will never win either; they are perpetually outgunned, literally and figuratively, and they have no better hope of a nation "from the river to the sea" than the descendants of the Iroquois have of reclaiming billion-dollar New York real estate. For now, activist zeal has returned, but the proponents of BDS and the dissolution of the Israeli ethnostate will never get what they want. Perhaps, for some, that is fine—the greatest motivator of activism is an unkillable foe—but for the genuine believers all of this will be a hard comedown. Israel won't budge. The United States and Western

Europe are committed to the status quo, and won't tolerate anything less.

The American Jew is not a terribly sympathetic figure here. I am not dodging rockets from the sky. I am writing comfortably, in New York City. My religion is, at best, a faint appendage of my greater self. It is more malleable than an ethnicity, but it has its own permanence, one suffused in culture. I take it with me and the antisemite reminds me of what it is, my little inheritance. I accept, too, the burdens of the nation I've called home, the one I pay taxes to, the one I will be a citizen of until death. If my patriotism is tepid, it is something that must be contemplated and ultimately contended with; it is worth having an argument about. On Israel, despite my many words on the subject, I find myself demanding a divorce between the nation and greater Jewry. Leave the diaspora alone. Or allow me my own fantasy: an army with which to quickly convince the Müllers and Kleinschmidts and Wagners that Zion belongs in the Rhineland or somewhere in the great middle of their country. Let the reparations be complete. Give Germany to the Jews and tell the Christ-worshipping Germans that France can be lovely this time of year, and that their fair skin should save them from the worst of the Frenchman's xenophobia. Jerusalem could be Berlin, or maybe Munich. Wherever the challah bread is better. I will make Aliyah there. I've never driven on the autobahn.

* * *

In November 2023, Columbia University announced they were suspending two student groups, Students for Justice in Palestine and Jewish Voice for Peace. The university stated, without going into further detail, that both groups "repeatedly violated" university policies related to holding campus events, culminating in an "unauthorized event" that went ahead "despite warnings and included threatening rhetoric and intimidation."

According to the *Columbia Spectator*, the student newspaper, the unauthorized event was a walkout that drew hundreds of students and included a "die-in" on the main plaza, where pro-Palestinian signs were waved, speakers denounced Israel's killing of Gazan civilians, and the protesters laid down across the plaza to symbolize the deaths. At one point, an unidentified person began screaming "antisemitic and anti-Black statements, then attempted to instigate fights with numerous students. The individual climbed over chains blocking off a grass area and continued yelling obscenities," the *Spectator* reported. "Students at the walkout booed the unidentified individual, and five confronted the individual while the speaker on the megaphone denounced antisemitism."

It was this, along with the groups' failure to apply for permits at least ten days in advance of any demonstration or protest, that apparently triggered the suspension, which lasted the rest of the fall term. In the interim, both SJP and JVP lost funding from the university administration.

Depending on your view of world events, this decision was either commendable or an abomination. It was, at the very minimum, proof that the Israel-Hamas war was not done roiling American institutions, which had shed their appetite for radical chic and returned to the relative conservatism that had been, until 2020, their default.

The immediate question to be asked was whether either of these student groups should have been suspended. If they continued to violate the school policy on applying for permits, no doubt there were sanctions that could have been meted out. But any pro-Palestinian activist was bound to wonder whether Columbia University, an elite institution funded by the wealthiest and most powerful families in America, would have shut down a Hillel organization or any other pro-Israel group that held a large, peaceful demonstration but didn't apply for a permit. While an antisemitic protester showed up at the Columbia die-in, the protest itself was not antisemitic—and, most importantly, it was devoid of violence. Students marched, spoke, and lay down. No one was punched, no windows were broken, no one was followed and harassed. Jewish students do feel unsafe on college campuses today and that fear must be taken seriously, but it can't be an excuse to shut down protest against the Israeli government. As much as unwavering Zionists and genuine antisemites strain to conflate Judaism with Israel, they are not, in fact, the same thing. Opposition to the policies of a nation-state is not opposition to an ancient religion. It's not as if everyone who follows Jesus Christ has to be accountable for the Papacy.

What was striking about the moment was how much had changed since 2020. In a little over three years, the most influential institutions in the worlds of academia, the arts, and multinational finance had evolved from fully genuflecting in front of zealous young activists to trying to silence and crush them. The difference, obviously, was the cause these activists had taken up. In 2020, the police killing of George Floyd sparked the largest mass protests since the civil rights movement. Marches for Floyd morphed into a general outcry against police brutality, and once marginal causes like defunding the police or exposing white fragility permeated the mainstream, championed by activists and institutions alike. It was the season of Amazon and Nike issuing tortured anti-racism statements and Nancy Pelosi and Chuck Schumer kneeling for almost nine minutes while wearing African kente cloth scarves. It was the season of the powerful being *afraid*, in some form, of the activist class, or at least feeling pressure to conform to their dictates. Much of it didn't age well, but some of it was well-intentioned enough. America really does incarcerate more people than any other country, the police do abuse the working class and poor, and racism hasn't vanished from this country. Enforcing new language norms in corporate boardrooms and Ivy League schools won't solve any of these problems, and when material needs are ignored, movements fail. Unlike in the civil rights era, the uprisings of 2020 didn't lead to sweeping policy changes. Today, few Democrats are campaigning on slashing police budgets.

If corporations and colleges had felt able to give ground on racial justice, they were not so willing to do the same for the Palestinians. Foreign conflicts can be more fraught than the domestic variety, but the reality is that there were few influential interest groups American institutions fretted about offending when they denounced Floyd's killing or printed anti-racism statements. It's not like Fox News or police unions have much purchase at Columbia. The donor class, pallidly liberal in their social outlook, could endorse justice for Floyd without fearing that their bottom line would be impacted. Israel is another matter entirely. It's easy enough to understand why a Jewish donor, Democrat or Republican, would be invested in Zionism and want to defend the Israeli government at all costs. Non-Jewish donors and administrators care too, in part because they view support for Israel as a bulwark against antisemitism—again, assuming the Netanyahu government is a stand-in for Judaism—and believe the ultimate aims of the Palestinian activists are too fringe. The Overton window moved much faster for defunding the police than for supporting pro-Palestinian activists. Calls for a single, multinational state—a democracy in the Middle East not predicated on upholding a majority of one religion or ethnicity—will not be humored by Columbia, Amazon, or anyone else.

Not all pro-Palestinian activists were asking for this explicitly, or even knew what it meant to demand a single state. Many were simply calling for a ceasefire—for Israel to stop bombarding Gaza in retaliation for the 1,200 Israelis killed, and hostages seized, by Hamas. The carnage was stunning. Tens of thousands of Palestinians dead, survivors starving, and the physical infrastructure of the Gaza Strip obliterated. Hamas, meanwhile, has not been defeated. Netanyahu talked of occupying Gaza indefinitely, waging a continuous war on the scale of the horrors America visited upon Iraq. This was all worth protesting, applying whatever pressure was possible on the Biden administration to bring Israel, effectively an American client state, to heel. Students at universities like Columbia do not have a direct line to the Biden White House. They can only do what their predecessors did during Vietnam: march and organize and protest until progress is made. Some protesters do oppose Zionism, and antisemites will always graft onto the anti-Zionist cause. But this doesn't mean every person marching for Palestinian dignity and an end to war hates Jews. In fact, leftist Jews are marching with them. There are Jews who are not Zionist at all.

Will speech rights survive the anti-Palestinian onslaught? In 2020, it was the left ignoring the tenets of free expression to enforce conformity around a rigid conception of racial justice and identity. Corporations were happy to play along. Now, critics of Israel face an even harsher crackdown, with the formerly woke and the Zionist anti-woke trying to stamp them out for good. The Trump administration, in 2025, began efforts to deport legal residents for criticizing Israel and cut funding to colleges that didn't sufficiently suppress pro-Palestine activists. College administrators and corporate titans don't care to posture for the Palestinians. BLM will not translate into PLM. And this made the clashes of 2023 and 2024 far more bitter, in a number of aspects, than anything that came to the fore in 2020, when a certain unanimity was forced into being. The generation gap was very real. If you're under forty, your only serious memory is of right-wing Israeli governments—various coalitions fronted by Netanyahu and the ultra-Orthodox, the sort of Jews who want not just to displace and annihilate the Palestinians but to ensure the Labor tradition in Israel is entirely erased. These governments want the West Bank occupied and the Rabin-endorsed Palestinian state to never have even a whisper of a chance of coming into being. Hamas, which openly longs for the destruction of Israel, is a convenient foil, every bit as maximalist as they are.

A fifty-, sixty-, or seventy-year-old might remember Golda Meir or a friendly kibbutz, or even the concept of the leftist Zionist—once, such a thing could exist. And they might remember the collections for Israel, planting a tree, the promise of making Aliyah. They do believe defending the Jews means defending Israel. For them, the youth, with their calls for BDS and liberation "from the river to the sea," are a true horror. They must be silenced. There is no *compromise* with them—just as the youth see no compromise, now, with their elders. Again, Vietnam comes to mind. The pro-war side recalled the glory and moral clarity of the Second World War, believing both could be transposed to another era. The baby boomers, then relative children, saw the dead Vietnamese babies. Israel was attacked first—the Vietnamese did not maraud through New York and Chicago, slaughtering with impunity—so this analogy can only go so far. Hamas, certainly, does not dream of the secularized democracy many activists hope for. It is exploiting Israel's savage overreach. But Israel's defenders should consider the untenable position they will soon find themselves in, absent any moral high ground. Shutting down JVP and SJP was a battle won. For the Israel hawks, the war will be much uglier.

It is easy to be cynical about Chuck Schumer, the Senate minority leader. Many years ago, when I profiled him for the *New York Observer*, I found a politician with few core convictions, a man willing to chase popularity at the expense of what might be right. Schumer supported the Iraq War and cheered on Wall Street through the 2008 crash. He rarely led and often followed. Unlike the late Harry Reid, who anointed the New York senator as his successor, Schumer didn't even command a political machine in his home state. Democrats win today in Nevada because of Reid, the ex-boxer from the town of Searchlight. In New York, the Democratic Party has been desiccated for decades.

On Israel, Schumer wasn't much different. If you are an Israel hawk, you had every reason to revere him until 2024. Whatever the Israeli government did—whether it was led, a long time ago, by Labor Zionists, or in recent times dominated by the far right—it was all fine with Schumer. Much of this was personal: Schumer built his political career in the Jewish neighborhoods of Brooklyn. He was born two years after Israel's founding, and he came up in politics when devotion to Zionism was as much a Democratic cause as a Republican one. The most liberal members of Congress, then, were arch-Zionists. There was a logic to this. Though Israel was founded on bloodshed, the Arabs expelled from their land, it was also, in its first decades, a country where the left wing held great power. For a decade-long stretch, from the late 1960s to the late 1970s, Labor dominated Israel, dramatically expanding the welfare state there. The party would fall from power but always come back. Yitzhak Rabin, who negotiated the Oslo Accords, belonged to Labor. Of course, he was assassinated, and the far right has been on the march in Israel since. Today, the Labor Party is effectively dead, and even the moderate coalition that briefly ousted Netanyahu couldn't hold on for long. Netanyahu is a political operator who goes where power is; he was able to become prime minister again by negotiating with the ultra-Orthodox and the revanchists, the sort who don't believe in any state for the Palestinians and would prefer them all exiled or dead.

Schumer stood on the floor of the Senate in 2024 and called for new elections in Israel. He called the Netanyahu government an obstacle to peace. He did not, as many activists had hoped, call for a permanent ceasefire or conditions on military aid. But it was easy to declare this a victory for the leftist, pro-Palestine activists in the United States—Jewish Voice for Peace, DSA, Within Our Lifetime, and the other assorted anti-Zionist groups—as well as the campaign to rack up "uncommitted" votes in various presidential primaries. Protest matters, particularly when it's sustained. Unlike Occupy Wall Street, pro-Palestine activism won't vanish, because the conflict itself, so tragic and unresolvable, won't quickly disappear from public view. There will be new atrocities to be enraged about, and the Netanyahu government is almost perfectly calibrated to enflame leftists in America and drive more liberals away from hardline Zionism. Schumer will be a Zionist until he dies, but his speech was extraordinary. It represented, in effect, the left-leaning Zionist's deep exhaustion with Netanyahu. And it proved the atrocities the Israeli government had committed since October 7—the ceaseless bombings, the starvation of civilians—were now outweighing, in the public's view, Hamas's initial slaughter.

Still, the pro-Palestine movement couldn't claim all credit for this reversal. Schumer disdained anti-Zionists. What mattered far more was Israel's conduct. The death toll of thirty thousand Gazans in the five months prior to Schumer's speech was almost unfathomable; it was the sort of death and destruction the twenty-first-century American government would only inflict over many years. It was more in line with Vietnam, or even the relentless civilian bombing campaigns in Japan that presaged Hiroshima and Nagasaki. The Republican hawks would never budge—Tom Cotton, Lindsey Graham, and Ted Cruz have built their political careers on calling for the destruction of various nations—but it put some of the Democratic Party's greatest Israel defenders in a bind. Ritchie Torres, a young goy congressman from New York City, grew into the most vocal Democratic Israel hawk in the House. AIPAC's most charismatic foot soldier, Torres was something of a parallel universe to AOC, a Puerto Rican born in the late 1980s who also represented the Bronx and had, through genuine ideological commitment or campaign donations or both, become Israel's staunchest defender on the left. Schumer and even Biden, to an extent, seemed discomfited by Israel's imminent invasion of Rafah. But Torres was a proud cheerleader for Israeli might.

The other great Israel hawk in the Democratic Party was Senator John Fetterman of Pennsylvania. Fetterman was once, like Torres, a Bernie Sanders supporter. To get elected in Pennsylvania, he aligned with progressives. In 2022, as he was facing down Dr. Oz, he steadily broke with them but still remained cordial. He was a soft Israel hawk then, not particularly outspoken about his foreign policy views because few asked. After the October 7 attacks, he became indistinguishable from Cruz, Cotton, and Graham. Unlike his colleagues in the Senate, particularly Chris Van Hollen of Maryland, he not only became a strident Netanyahu backer but repeatedly mocked anyone who dared question the Israeli military's decisions. The same sophomoric, 2010s-style Gawkerspeak that won him so many plaudits on the left when he was savaging a TV doctor now proved alienating because it was aimed almost exclusively at anyone who was pro-Palestine. More intriguing was that both Fetterman and Torres, like AIPAC, were operating to the right of Schumer. Until 2024, Schumer was a Democrat fully in AIPAC's fold. He spoke at their conferences, took their money, and towed their line. Torres was a congressman in Schumer's city with a constituency that was either deeply indifferent to Israel—the Latinos of the Bronx—or, in the case of one particularly affluent neighborhood (Riverdale), supportive, but more in the way Schumer may have been: Zionist forever, but wondering how many Gazans, exactly, have to die for October 7.

If the constituency for the anti-Zionists who longed for Israel to collapse into dust—or at least evolve into a binational state with no Jewish majority—was very small, it was hard to see who the mass audience for the Fetterman- and Torres-style Democrats could be. Republicans at least had the excuse of pandering to the evangelicals, who are influential within the GOP and have their own biblical reasons for backing Israel in every war. Fetterman and Torres could each say they represented Jews—Philadelphia and Pittsburgh have plenty, and a small slice of Torres's district contains some Orthodox—but there are very few Americans who support one foreign nation unconditionally. Orthodox Jews are a vanishingly small slice of the national electorate. Even if the polls, forevermore, were to show more Americans backed Israel than the Palestinians, they would always display nuance. There was nothing radical about suggesting America shouldn't hand out blank checks for military weaponry to a nation that had shown little interest in preventing civilian deaths. There was nothing radical about suggesting Israel's relationship to the United States shouldn't be beyond criticism—it's not as if France or Lithuania or India could perpetually escape all opprobrium. The political bent of Israel will eventually make the old American foreign policy consensus unsustainable, especially for future Democratic presidents. Biden, like Schumer, had a lifetime steeped in Israel advocacy. He remembered Labor Zionism. For those that don't, they see Israel for what it is—a nation captured by its retrograde right. All of this will make speeches like Schumer's more common and the Fetterman approach increasingly alienating. Schumer is a political weathervane; he represents, almost perfectly, the median Democrat. This is how, in part, he's remained an elected official for fifty years. He has rarely led, but he's never been too far behind.

Torres himself believed nothing had changed after Schumer's speech. And he wasn't entirely wrong. Biden did nothing to forestall carnage in Gaza. He neither placed conditions on US military aid nor exercised American leverage. He was never going to go as far as Schumer and call for a new prime minister. Democrats who may run for president in the future, though, took note of the speech. The likes of Torres and Fetterman will not own the future of the party. There will be fewer and fewer Democratic presidential candidates who talk like the congressman from the Bronx and the senator from Pennsylvania. Israel is squandering its political capital in America. Schumer, who took stock of it more than almost anyone alive, understood this well. Someday, the other hawks might too.

6

Culture

Cultural upheavals are a riddle in real time. Trends that might seem obvious in hindsight are poorly understood in the present or not fathomed at all. The 2024 presidential election came after Covid-19 had killed millions and, for a period, reordered existence as we knew it. Perhaps more than any other crisis in modern times, the pandemic marked a new era, the world of the 2010s wrenched away for good.

The future cannot be known—not with so much war and political instability, the rise of autocrats across the world, and the Trumpian disruptions. Within the roil—or below it—one could hazard, at least, a hypothesis: a change had arrived and needed to be named. A rebellion both conscious and unconscious had begun. It was happening both online and off, and the *off* was where the youth may have preferred to wage it. It echoed, in its own way, a great shift that came more than two centuries earlier, out of the ashes of the Napoleonic Wars.

A new romanticism arrived, butting up against and even outright rejecting the empiricism that had reigned for a significant chunk of this century. Backlash was bubbling against tech's dominance of everyday life, particularly the godlike algorithms—their true calculus still proprietary—that rule all of digital existence.

The famed mantra of the liberal left in the early months of the pandemic—*trust the science*—faded from view, as hero worship ceased for the bureaucrat scientists (Dr. Anthony Fauci) and even for the pharmaceutical behemoths that had developed, with federal assistance, the Covid vaccines.

Church attendance, long the barometer of America's devotion to the unseen, continued to plummet, but what was taking its place wasn't the pugnacious New Atheism that had tugged at the discourse for a stretch of the 2000s. Instead, it was what could be loosely termed "spirituality"—a devotion to astrology, witchcraft, magic, and manifestation that emerged, particularly among the young. Online life, paradoxically enough, only catalyzed this spirituality further, with teenage TikTok occultists and "manifesting" influencers racking up ever more followers.

All of this, as the writer and music historian Ted Gioia argued in 2023, might have been inevitable, given the societal disruption of the last two decades. On Christmas Day 2003, Facebook, Instagram, YouTube, X (Twitter), and TikTok did not exist. Google was merely a popular search engine competing with the likes of Netscape Navigator for market share. Amazon had not eviscerated the bricks-and-mortar shopping giants of the twentieth century. There was no such thing as an iPhone;

cellphones were not ubiquitous, and they could only be used for calls and texts.

Online life back then was clearly cleaved away from where one actually conducted a social existence: gossiping with friends, shopping at the mall, and congregating in physical groups to play video games. "Surfing the web" was a distinct activity undertaken at a desktop computer. It had, each day, an obvious beginning and end.

The digital explosion would forever change how we view the world and interact with one another. The late 2000s were characterized by what might have been the last burst of techno-optimism for decades to come. Facebook was credited, in part, for helping to elect Barack Obama, the first Black president, and the new social media and its attendant smartphone technology was treated with a kind of messianic reverence. "Learn to code" was the mantra of the age, STEM the only ticket to the American dream. When Steve Jobs died in 2011, it was like another Gandhi had left us, and the existence of Apple itself was regarded as an unalloyed blessing.

Trump's shock election in 2016 would permanently alter how Facebook was perceived—it was no longer merely a proving ground for the young liberal vanguard—and other social media platforms became increasingly terrifying places to come of age. Instagram wrecked body images, smartphones metastasized schoolyard bullying into a 24/7 enterprise, and teen depression, even before the arrival of Covid, surged.

Adults weren't much better off. For thousands of years, mature human beings knew how to be alone with their own thoughts and to tolerate boredom. The smartphone's addictive entertainments destroyed attention spans. The market, meanwhile, was suddenly glutted with underemployed computer science and business majors. Surging interest rates strangled the startup economy. There would be no Uber 2.0.

None of this, by now, was new. But the 2020s romanticism was—though it may have mirrored what came long before. In the early years of the nineteenth century, rationalism seemed ascendant, as the rapid technological changes brought about by the Industrial Revolution promised their own algorithmic models for daily life. Machines displaced the old craftsmen and the workers that remained were punished through all their waking hours, forced to meet productivity goals that would have been science fiction a generation before. The individual, flesh-and-blood human never meant less, now that wonders like the cotton gin and the coal-fired steam engine could accomplish so much.

Romanticism was the great, bloody cry against it all. Luddites began by burning factories to the ground. Artists declared war on the principles of the Age of Reason that had seemed to beget the new industrial drudgery. Mary Shelley's *Frankenstein* offered a frightening riposte to those who believed science would deliver only bountiful good. Beethoven unleashed radical symphonies of a sweep and emotional intensity hitherto unknown in Western music. The English novelist Ann Radcliffe wrote a prescient defense of terror as a literary device, as the Gothic—dark swallowing light—rushed back into vogue.

The poets and painters, the influencers of their age, lashed the old gods of logic and gentility. William Wordsworth and Samuel Taylor Coleridge blasted away at British cultural elites in *Lyrical Ballads*; Percy Bysshe Shelley and Lord Byron lurched between profound ecstasy and crepuscular sorrow in their poetry. William Blake, beset by visions of trees glittering with angels, believing the imagination was the most vital element of human existence, became the herald for generations of metaphysical insurgents and revolutionaries. Ralph Waldo Emerson lectured about the invisible eyeball and the over-soul.

Not all of the old romantics were opposed to Judeo-Christian religion, but they were drawn, like the youth of the twenty-first century, to spiritual realms that operated far beyond any biblical teachings or rationalist precepts. They were deeply wary of technology's encroachment on the human spirit. They feared, ultimately, an inhuman future—hence their rebellion. Today's romantics, still nascent, sense something similar. Why else, in such an algorithmic and data-clogged age, with so much of existence quantifiable and knowable, would magic suddenly hold such sway?

The greater hope for the new romanticism is, in some sense, art—not the dominance of digital charlatans who promise all of life's riches if only you visualize hard enough or utter the correct incantations. Embracing the paranormal or believing wholeheartedly that star positions determine personalities can be harmless fun—until the delusions become life-consuming and despair takes hold when they inevitably fail to deliver on their promise.

Irrationality, on its own, is no virtue, and some of the romantics of the nineteenth and twenty-first centuries succumb to the same ancient dross—magic alone as the supposed channel to transcendence. That spiritualism has spread with tech is an irony fitting of the age.

There was logic, though, in the anti-logic. Science is science, not a religion, but for many months in 2020 and 2021 it was treated as one, even as the scientists failed, in several striking instances, to adequately explain or predict the behavior of the virus in our midst. Masks were ineffective and a waste of money, until they weren't; the vaccines were a miracle cure that would immediately stop the spread of Covid, until the virus kept circulating anyway. Fauci was a cult hero who nevertheless became the face of a shambolic pandemic response, his mythos swelling with the nation's death toll.

Trust in the science did not curdle at the same instant as trust in the tech conglomerates, but they are not so dissimilar when weighed against the hype of progress. The new romantics wonder: What good has any of this done for us? Were the hyper-sophisticated GPS devices, cameras, and video recorders worth it? It is too soon to predict a revival of the Luddites, but there has been at least one press report of a teen group ditching smartphones altogether because "social media and phones are not real life."

Science brought about these revolutions; science compressed once unimaginable computing power into a single handheld device. Science now promises a great leap forward with artificial intelligence, which seems intent on replacing the arts themselves—machines will now make mediocre art, music, literature, and even fact-challenged journalism.

The amusement phase had passed. The modern creative class—barraged by two decades of digital technology that had radically chcapened music, television and cinema—was ready for combat, as the successful writers' and actors' strikes of 2023 demonstrated. But rapacious tech still had a mass buy-in. Smartphones were ubiquitous. Facebook, Apple, Amazon, and Google were hegemonic. Mark Zuckerberg sculpted his pharaonic Hawaiian compound. Reid Hoffman cut enormous checks to Kamala Harris's presidential campaign. They owned the present. But whether they owned the future was no longer obvious. Generational change is hard on the incumbents. And romanticism wouldn't hold still: it promised, at the minimum, a wild and unsteady flame. What it ended up burning was still anyone's guess.

As 2024 loomed, the wider culture was increasingly divorced from presidential politics. Apart from Israel and Palestine, and the assassination attempt on Trump,

America witnessed little like the hyperpolitics of the 2010s and 2020, when most of cultural life seemed to be filtered through what Trump said, did, and thought. It was good that national politics no longer defined, so aggressively, what we watched, listened to, and read. A healthy nation must periodically compartmentalize. This was one benefit of the Biden era.

Ted Gioia posited that, at the start of the election year, the macroculture and the microculture would go to war. Another astute cultural writer, Mo Diggs, identified the mesoculture as what America most lacks, and what we might require to recover both stability and sanity. As implied in its name, the macroculture is still what most Americans think of today when they imagine who produces the music, the movies, the news, the books—all that *content*, to wield a dreaded term. Hollywood, of course, is the macroculture. Disney and Paramount reign above, along with tech giants like Amazon and Apple who have made significant incursions into the entertainment space. Spotify and Netflix are the macro streamers. The major record conglomerates, including Sony Music Group and Universal Music Group, belong here, as does all of legacy media. The *New York Times*, the *Atlantic*, and the *New Yorker* are the macroculture, as are 20th Century Studios (Disney), Fox News, ABC News (Disney), ESPN (Disney), CNN (Warner Bros. Discovery), NBC, CBS (Paramount), and HBO (Warner Bros. Discovery). Corporate publishers and their imprints all belong, too. Size alone isn't the determinant of what resides in the macroculture. Smaller newspapers and online publications like *Slate* and *Vox* can be considered macro in sentiment. Most magazines are the same way.

The macroculture is both extraordinarily wealthy and uniquely vulnerable. The second part of this formulation was not true until the twenty-first century, when the internet matured and obliterated, at once, several remarkably durable business models. When the macroculture was on sturdier financial ground, Americans benefited more, in part because there was a greater degree of narrative diversity. Mainstream cinema could, at any given time, feature action films, rom-coms, high-concept art films, historical epics, psychological thrillers, regular comedies, and original IP franchises. In the 1980s, 1990s, and 2000s, there were many types of tentpole films. But as Hollywood grew vulnerable over the last decade and a half—with more and more consumers shifting to streaming and staying home—the retread culture, which still strangles us today, emerged: superhero films, films based on video games, films owed entirely to ancient intellectual property. As good as *Barbie* was, this was the ultimate problem with a film featuring a doll first sold in 1959, a full decade before men walked on the moon. There was no new doll, no new flying hero or righteous mutant, no fresh IP. Thirty years ago, the macroculture cared far more about newness.

It is harder to generalize about book publishing because so many different kinds of works get published every year, even if they are marginalized by a public that mostly doesn't read them. But I'll speak, in broad strokes, to the general culture of literary fiction, which held a kind of prestige in the twentieth century that it may never recapture. Arguably, when there was less conglomeration in publishing, a wider array of novels reached the broader public. Writers themselves could be regional, class-based, highly educated, or completely bereft of elite formal schooling. Many more of them came from the working class. The moneyed coasts, East and West, always exerted the biggest pull, but there were many different schools and styles, and even politics, taking root in the vast middle of the country. And it wasn't just the middle: within coastal cities themselves, like New York and Los Angeles, tribunes for the alienated and the destitute could more readily emerge. Outsiders like Samuel Delany, Hubert Selby Jr., and Flannery O'Connor still barreled their way into the macroculture and were even exalted there. I don't want to idealize all of this too much—we are a less racist country today, and twentieth-century publishing had many failings—but the discontent a reader might feel in the 2020s is connected to all those novels conceived, almost entirely, in one milieu: upper-middle-class affluence within a fashionable metropolitan area. These worlds are usually white, but they don't have to be, and what left-liberals never quite understand is that there is far more solidarity between a Black Swarthmore graduate and a white Swarthmore graduate than between a white attorney from Grosse Pointe and a white Dollar General clerk in the Lansing exurbs. The literary novels that achieve widest distribution today are, with some exceptions, preoccupied with the struggles and neuroses of those wielding the most cultural capital.

The major record labels, meanwhile, struggle to break out big stars. Taylor Swift wasn't readily supplanted. The A&R functionaries race desperately to recruit the new stalwarts of the microculture as hitmakers, throwing out record deals to anyone who seems to achieve a moment of virality. They don't nurture talent or understand, really, how to distribute it outward. This is mostly—but not entirely—their fault; the internet wrecked every distribution channel imaginable, from the record store to the music magazine, and MTV has lost all relevance. Radio stations no longer distinguish themselves in any regional market. Drive through Chicago or Oakland or Buffalo and you will hear the exact same songs on any local affiliate—if you're listening at all.

Much has been written already on the fracturing of culture and our dwindling consensus zones—no *Friends* or *Seinfeld* for Americans to gather around every Thursday evening. This has long been a challenge for the macroculture, and it will only get worse in the coming years. The theme here is financial struggle: most of the conglomerates and media properties aren't as wealthy as they once were. The bleeding out of the large newspapers, the regional newspapers, and the digital insurgents alike is well known, with an obvious enough culprit.

The print advertising model was never replaced. What has been surprising, as we reach the midpoint of the current decade, is how some of the storied incumbents can't even garner attention anymore. The 2010s riddle was how to monetize interest. More dire, for a vaunted institution like the *Washington Post*, is that half of its traffic has vanished since 2020. Traffic itself is virtually worthless, but it is a barometer that can't be ignored entirely.

The walls between the cultures can be porous. Many in the microculture still long for the prestige of the macro and, perhaps, its cash. If not ignoring it altogether, the macrocultural players look upon the micro with a mixture of wariness and envy, wondering how it booms while they experience little other than retrenchment. Individuals like Joe Rogan may shuttle from one culture to the other and back again. Rogan first found fame as a comedian and the host of *Fear Factor*, firmly situated in the macroculture. He then became far more famous, and richer, in the microculture, launching one of the most popular podcasts in the world and streaming it on YouTube. The macroculture took notice: after Spotify paid him more than $200 million, he became the object of both scorn and genuine fascination in the mainstream media.

The macroculture, it must be emphasized, is nowhere near collapse. I think it will transmogrify rather than vanish. But it's no longer growing. It's the microculture that's expanding, often explosively. This is not a value judgement, merely a bare fact.

In the United States, the cultural undercurrent of Israel's war against Hamas and its catastrophic siege of Gaza was the ideological cleavage between the old and the young. If you were under thirty-five you conceived of Israel as an oppressor state, and the sins of Hamas as secondary to seventy-five years of colonialism. If you were older, you might have been disconcerted by the civilian casualties in Gaza but believe, ultimately, that Israel has a right to defend itself against terrorism—or, at least, that Zionism itself is not evil.

TikTok has harbored the most pro-Palestine and anti-Israel sentiment, leading to accusations that the Chinese-run social media giant is catalyzing an entire generation against Israel through the manipulation of algorithms. Jewish celebrities fumed that TikTok might even have been responsible, in some form, for the Hamas attacks. Much of this thinking was simplistic, since young, left-leaning Americans don't need social media in order to care about the bombing of Gaza. And Hamas doesn't need social media in order to hate Israel. But it is inarguable that TikTok platformed more anti-Israel voices because its success was built on decentralization: anyone can create a TikTok video, and gatekeepers, theoretically, are nonexistent.

TikTok is best understood as one of the most famous and successful components of the microculture. Even if its growth is slowing and the metrics of virality can be nebulous, it is a platform that is, for now at least, capturing the greatest share of youth attention. It embodies the microculture because it is bottom-up, not top-down; macrocultural luminaries can be successful on TikTok, but popularity percolates differently, and its celebrities might be rich without the attendant trappings of the old macrocultural fame, that lost world of Empire. Instagram works similarly: owned by Facebook, a macrocultural titan, yet fueled entirely by the attention of the individual users who fill it, free of charge, with all of its content.

In terms of raw growth, the greater success story of the microculture might be the Google-owned YouTube. Its top creators are perpetually expanding. MrBeast has soared past 100 million subscribers, with his rate of growth still increasing. Forty-three YouTube channels attract more than a half billion views a month. Stripe, the payment processor for most online transactions, revealed that the so-called creator economy—those in the microculture using online platforms—has continually expanded over the last two years. In 2021, Stripe aggregated data from fifty popular creator platforms and found they had added 668,000 creators, who received a combined total of $10 billion in payouts. In 2023, those same fifty platforms had added over 1 million creators and paid out more than $25 billion in earnings.

The context here is the timeframe. The early 2020s were a bloodbath for macrocultural media. Other than, perhaps, the *New York Times*, there were no success stories. Disney stock plunged. Cable ratings evaporated. Post-Trump news traffic dried up. Netflix suddenly realized there was no pot of gold at the end of the streaming rainbow.

Images and video don't rule the entirety of the microculture. Substack, for instance, belongs to the micro, as blogs did in the 2000s before they were subsumed by social media and larger websites, or undone by the lack of dollars available to those who wrote for the web. Substack cannot replace the newspapers that have collapsed, or replicate the alternative media ecosystem that has mostly been destroyed. What it does offer is a way for some to either make a comfortable living or partial living from writing or, absent that, at least hunt out a fresh audience bored by what the macroculture has been disgorging over the last few years. Stripe is what makes Substack, for writers like me, viable; it's easy for those who want to support me to pay for what I write, thus solving the great dilemma of the old blogs, which could not, for the most part, convert readers into paying customers.

What is intriguing about Substack is what is intriguing about modern-day YouTube: growth. As with any online platform, there is a tremendous divide between the enormously popular and the anonymous, but a Substack middle class is slowly taking root as newsletters continually add new readers. There is no such thing as a *Washington Post*–style crisis, where an audience evaporates. The opposite is true, with those who put the work in getting rewarded with new subscribers. Whatever the pace, the numbers keep going up, not down. A knock against Substack is that the macrocultural heavyweights who end up there merely replicate their success; this is partially true. Matt Taibbi was a fairly famous *Rolling Stone* correspondent, Matt Yglesias had a large social media following from two decades of blogging, and Bari Weiss had sinecures at the *Times* and the *Wall Street Journal*. While all of that aids in success, none of it guarantees large audiences will follow. Some have leapt from the legacy media to Substack and found, in fact, that they can't make it entirely work. And other Substack titans had no fame before migrating over to the newsletter service. Heather Cox Richardson was a history professor at Boston College, known chiefly in academic circles. The aforementioned Ted Gioia, who is nearing 100,000 subscribers on his own Substack, was known to jazz enthusiasts but didn't boast a significant social media presence or decades spent on cable television. Anne Kadet, a New York–based journalist, shot past 10,000 subscribers in two short years by conducting quirky interviews and cultural excavations of the kind that the macroculture would ignore. The thrill of Substack is the sheer diversity of voices: racial, ideological, cultural, and political. It is something of an underground press, diffuse and raffish and maybe more ambitious. If only it could all be fused together into a neo–*Village Voice*, stuffed into a news box every week.

In the last century, the macrocultural elites would try to glom onto, appropriate, or make a study of the microcultural equivalent of their day: the counterculture. Hollywood, the large publishing houses, and Madison Avenue were all deeply interested in the protest movements, the new rock music, and the aesthetics of the baby boomer set, in part because they wanted to ensure all of it could be properly commodified. And the creators within the macro, the mainstream, wanted to learn—they were interested in advancement and innovation for its own sake, the desire to reimagine what was possible. New Hollywood, postmodernist literature, and the rising sophistication of network television were all reflective of this shift. The counterculture strengthened the mainstream.

Today, the relationship is far more fraught. Most macrocultural operators remain befuddled by Substack, wishing it all would go away or drown in its mostly nonexistent problems. CNN, the *Atlantic*, and NPR won't set up on Substack. And when media conglomerates do poach YouTubers or podcasters from the microculture, as in the cases of McAfee or Lilly Singh, they hope the amorphous formats of their prior productions can be jammed into the structured world of television. Macrocultural elites rarely, though, try to learn from the success of what's churning below, or how rapid growth is still possible when so much of the mainstream seems to be contracting. The trouble, too, is that the tech behemoths rely on the microculture for their own survival and no longer innovate themselves. The relationship is, if not vampiric, then feudal: Google controls

YouTube, Facebook controls Instagram, Elon Musk controls X, ByteDance controls TikTok, and the creators themselves till the digital fields, tirelessly generating value for their bosses while hoping some of it gets kicked back to them. At some point, this tension will break out into the open, as all of these platforms, in various forms, try to demonetize or suppress the content they do not like. Palestinian voices will find TikTok less hospitable in the coming months and years. The new platforms Big Tech tries to create will not help either. Threads cannot replace Twitter because it hates the written word.

The microculture, though, is not an ideal because it is still a realm of haves and have-nots. Most people are not MrBeast or even a sliver of a fraction of MrBeast. Most people cannot crowdfund $1 million for their fantasy novel. Most people cannot pay their rent with a Substack or Patreon income. There is the risk, like with the oversaturation of podcasts, that too many creators will go begging in front of the same audiences and monetary returns will diminish.

What we need is more than a macroculture and a microculture; what thrived in the late twentieth and early twenty-first centuries and is now dissipating.

The cultural producers—painters, musicians, writers, actors, filmmakers, and podcasters—can feel alienated today because neither the macroculture nor the microculture are terribly hospitable. The macroculture has mostly stopped innovating or nurturing new talent, and it denies a middle-class existence to many would-be creators because so many different business models are going bust. There was a time when a mortgage could be paid off by working as a reporter at a midsized newspaper in a city like Cleveland or Denver. Or a writer who had an interest in the arts could get paid by one of these newspapers, on a regular basis, to review new novels, art exhibitions, movies, or albums. To make art, criticize art, or practice journalism in this precarious time often requires a degree of family support or outside wealth that is not available to the poor, the working class, or even some in the middle.

There are opportunities in the microculture, but far less stability. And for those who have no great interest in TikTok or YouTube, the cultural horizons can seem circumscribed. The aesthetics of both platforms may lack appeal. In a war between Hollywood and TikTok, are any of us winners?

Mo Diggs described the mesoculture as a 2000s phenomenon with antecedents in the 1980s and '90s. It was indie rock, underground hip-hop, small press literature, the blogs, and the last of the alternative newspapers. It was what was too small for the macroculture, and perhaps too offline to be entirely micro. As the counterculture waned, the mesoculture stepped in, and then the social media age swallowed it all. The streaming model, concurrently, further undercut the major labels of the macroculture while weakening the music blogs and websites like Pitchfork that wielded tangible influence just outside the mainstream. Algorithms took precedent over hipster critics. The apotheosis of the mesoculture might have been 2009, when indie rock darlings Grizzly Bear played a concert that Jay-Z attended and later gushed about:

> I hope this happens because it will push rap, it will push hip-hop to go even further—what the indie rock movement is doing right now is very inspiring. It felt like us in the beginning. These concerts, they're not on the radio, no one hears about them, and there's 12,000 people in attendance.

It was the same year Animal Collective, an experimental psychedelic and folk band that was my favorite in college, released an album that peaked at no. 13 on the Billboard charts. Several years before, buzz from music blogs had made the band Clap Your Hands Say Yeah enough of a cultural phenomenon that one of their songs appeared in *The Office*.

My bias is toward indie rock, but the mesoculture is about more than bands you might find too obscure or twee. It is what lies in between, as well as the demand for physical communion. The microculture is relentlessly online. As bountiful as Substack might be, it is not a newspaper office or a DIY show. It is not a raucous debate at a coffee shop. Pro-Palestine TikTok content is nothing compared to the rush of an actual street protest, of which there are many now. Slowly, the mesoculture crawls back. The recent burst of new literary journals and magazines represents one element in a small resurgence. Dimes Square, though derided, was a grasp at building the mesoculture. *County Highway*, a print-only nationwide newspaper, is amassing a readership. Post-pandemic, there is a greater longing for readings, performances, and parties. Five hundred people or more will attend a literary launch. What is missing, still, is the larger alternative infrastructure, particularly newspapers, which can no longer sustain themselves. *The Voice* has no print edition. The *Boston Phoenix* is dead, as is the *Baltimore City Paper*. Substack newsletters do not yet sway the zeitgeist like the blogs of twenty years ago did. Yet if the mesoculture grows more vibrant, the macroculture will be forced to respond. A half century ago, the counterculture revolutionized much of the machinery above it, and someday a new mesoculture could do the same. It will expand, regardless, because it is needed. The yearning, among enough younger Americans, is there. Most online platforms amount to empty calories, and so much of digital life ends up antic or glum. There is only so much posting to be done. Meanwhile, the macro mandarins have to figure out how to staunch the bleeding. Retreads, mergers, and pivots to video won't do it. They'll have to start imagining again.

7

The Election

For Democrats, the presidential race was probably lost on the night of the 2022 midterms.

It was then, against the headwinds of history, Democrats grew their Senate majority. It was then that they performed far better in House races than initially forecasted. It was then that they believed they had a glorious plan for victory: stump on abortion rights and warn, repeatedly, of Donald Trump's potential to destroy democracy as we know it.

President Joe Biden, about to turn eighty, was emboldened. If there were whispers that he should not seek another term, they were silenced that night. His party had won. He was in command. He had crushed Trump once, and he would do so again. His advisers formed an impenetrable wall around him.

Any talk of age-related diminishment was savagely dismissed—and then Team Biden barreled forward, into disaster.

Biden, of course, would eventually drop out of the race. But his departure and the euphoria surrounding the sudden rise of Kamala Harris obscured a reality that Democratic elites were far too quick to ignore: It was an intractable problem that Harris did not have to win a single vote in a primary. It had been more than a half century since any major party nominee was decided that way.

And it was Biden's fault, ultimately, that Harris ascended in such a fashion. He wanted a second term badly enough that he wasted the entire primary season running for a nomination he would never claim. His ego blinded him and his myopic advisers enabled a foolhardy campaign. He guaranteed Harris—and only Harris—was the only option for the Democratic Party trying once more to defeat Trump.

Would a different Democrat have won the popular vote and the Electoral College? We'll never know. But open primaries are effective sorting mechanisms. The best presidential candidates are forged in them. Barack Obama had to surge past Hillary Clinton in 2008. He was not the preferred choice of the Democratic establishment.

He barnstormed across the country and took control of the future, if he's no great shakes anymore. His surrogate work failed. Trump left his multiracial coalition in tatters. His hectoring of nonwhite men didn't boost Harris very much.

Biden, in 2022, should have quit while he was ahead. He should have announced he was not seeking another term and fulfilled the implicit promise of his 2020 campaign, which was building a bridge to a much younger generation of Democrats. He was plainly incapable of waging a vigorous campaign in 2024. He had a chance, right at the midterms, to permit an open primary to replace him.

Perhaps Harris, the sitting vice president, wins that primary anyway. If so, she would have at least been forced to craft a compelling rationale for her candidacy. She would have had to have gone to states like South Carolina, Michigan, and Georgia to explain why, exactly, she wanted to be president and what she might do if she assumed the most powerful office in the history of mankind. A primary would have compelled her, above all, to have a message.

Few voters understood what Harris wanted out of the Oval Office. *We're not going back* wasn't enough. Trump, for all his lies and inanities, had an obvious, digestible message for the voters of the seven swing states that decided the election. He wanted to drastically curtail immigration, slap tariffs on imports, combat inflation, and wind down so-called "forever" wars.

Many of these promises lacked detail. But it's crucial that they existed in the first place. They formed, together, a worldview that could either be accepted or rejected.

Candidate quality matters, and Harris, for all the joy she inspired, had a horrendous electoral track record. In 2019, she ran for president and performed so poorly she had to exit the race before the Iowa caucuses. Andrew Yang outpolled her and Tulsi Gabbard, who has since left the Democratic Party, outdebated her. She would have remained a senator from California were it not for

Biden's decision to add her to the ticket in 2020. Suddenly, a failed presidential candidate who had also, in her lone competitive statewide race, barely triumphed was now a leader of the Democratic Party.

A 2024 primary could have at least tested Harris's mettle. The Democrats had no shortage of capable candidates who wanted the nomination. There were a bevy of swing state senators and governors, as well as other prominent elected officials, ready to compete. Any one of them could have broken through, or Harris, in victory, would have engaged with millions of Democratic voters and been better for it. She would not have been such a muddle.

That's the danger of foregoing primaries. That's the danger of hoping democracy can be sidestepped. It is true that incumbent parties across the world have been battered, and inflation, as a global phenomenon, would have eaten into Harris's margins no matter what she did. It's also true, as the sitting vice president, that she was the de facto incumbent. She could not plausibly break from Biden. A different Democrat would have been better positioned to pull off that trick.

Now Democrats, as in 2016, are staring into the abyss. This time, as in 2004, they have lost the popular vote, a resounding rejection that should trigger a reassessment of all that they do and how, in the first place, they approach the American electorate. Some of this will be sorted out in the next open Democratic primary, which will take place in 2028. Some liberals believe fascism is near, and that they've voted in their last free election. This is deeply wrong and also defeatist. Democracy will continue to exist. It simply offers no promise for particular electoral outcomes. It does not guarantee someone like Trump can't win. In fact, it creates the possibility for men like him to rise. He won more votes this time.

When that presidential primary is held, Democrats will have their strongest standard-bearer—the one who has the will of the party's electorate behind them.

After the election I was struggling to remember what Barack Obama had done since he left the White House. To challenge myself, I decided not to look anything up and truly disgorge whatever images and ideas had been lodged in my memory. There was the jetting around with Richard Branson. There was a podcast of some sort, a Netflix documentary (or documentaries), a chat with Bruce Springsteen. There's the summer reading list. His wife published a book that outsold even his own. He campaigned, of course, for other Democrats, whether it was candidates in the midterms or Joe Biden, his successor. In 2024, he and Michelle delivered speeches at the Democratic National Convention that were extraordinarily well-received. I did think, and still do, that if either had run in this race against Donald Trump, they could have won.

None of that matters because the Constitution bars Barack from serving again and Michelle has no interest. They both stumped for Kamala Harris and had nothing to show for it. As Black men bled out of the Democratic coalition, Obama hectored them on the campaign trail for making "excuses" about not wanting a female president. It was professorial Obama at his finest; no hope, no change, merely condemnation for not doing what better-educated elders expected of you. Not surprisingly, few listened to him, and Trump proceeded to annihilate the multiracial Democratic coalition that Obama had assembled in two stunningly successful presidential runs. In 2016, Hillary Clinton was able to cling to bits of what Obama had left behind—she was still running up the score in Miami-Dade County and dominating along the Rio Grande—and Biden in 2020 grasped at less of it, benefiting more from an anti-Trump turnout boom that sent him to the White House. Politically and culturally, the Obamas found themselves in a transformed nation, the zeitgeist hurrying past them. The youngest generations, veering rightward, have little regard for them, and aging Democrats are beginning to think of Obama, as the writer Ethan Strauss pointed out, as a Michael Jordan–like presence: the greatest there ever was, but mostly disconnected to the present day. Barack Obama is a symbol, a monument. Like all ex-presidents, this is his fate, and when he's trundling about doing his surrogate work in 2028, it will be as a specter of what was and will probably not be again. There will be other Democratic presidents, but there won't be another Obama.

The dismantling of the Obama coalition—the great

surge of new, nonwhite voters into the Republican Party—doesn't have to be permanent. Trump's victory resembles George W. Bush's in 2004, when he also won the popular vote and was supported by more than 40 percent of Latinos. Two years later, a backlash midterm made Nancy Pelosi speaker, and two years after that, America elected its first Black president. American politics is fickle and fluid; coalitions are made to be broken, and loyalty to party is barely skin-deep.

These are dark times for the liberal left—for its media organs, politicians, writers, and thought leaders. Eight years ago, Trump could be dismissed as an aberration. The anti-fascist industry boomed. It was easy, since Trump did not win the popular vote, to call him illegitimate. Autocrats do not stay in power by winning free and fair elections, and the Electoral College is plainly an antiquated mechanism for picking leaders. There was great bile and rage over an election being, in the view of some, *stolen*—stolen by institutions that allegedly enabled a racist, rural right wing—and it helped that a foreign power was possibly involved. An inverse Cold War dynamic bloomed, with liberals emerging as neo–Cold Warriors against a Russian incursion and Trump Republicans defending the Vladimir Putin regime. There were marches—so many marches—and endless calls to action that radiated with self-satisfaction. This was the era of performing woe as publicly as possible and aligning yourself, as desperately as you could, with the de rigueur causes. There was a season for everything:

#MeToo, defund the police, save the immigrants. New celebrities were minted overnight. Alexandria Ocasio-Cortez might have been a democratic socialist, but she was a triumph, stylistically, of the liberal left, and she made it clear it was identity that would be centered first and always.

Why didn't they listen? This is the anguished cry of the liberal media critic who was sure the *New York Times*, despite its anti-Trump alignment, had perniciously normalized Trump. This is the cry, too, of the *Times* opinion page, of elite academia, of the *Atlantic* set, of the staffers at the *Washington Post* who longed for a Kamala Harris endorsement, and the many ponderous *New Yorker* writers with their grayish, interchangeable prose. This is the cry of a Democratic National Committee so sure, after the 2022 midterms, there was nothing more to do than call Trump a fascist ten thousand additional times—if only then, those dolts in Bucks County would listen. And it was Harris herself, feinting toward Obama, who would somehow deliver a mandate absent a single primary vote. There is a style here that might have to be left in 2024: that of the professionalized, practiced, technocratic politician in possession of two selves, one affixed like a plastic shell over the viscous guts where the truth lies. This is show business. Trump is a showman, but he does not do show business. He is raw, crude, hilarious, and disgusting, utterly unchanged by his settings. The lesson of Trump is not necessarily to *be* Trump. The lesson, simply, is to be as you are, and if you've got a raw charisma, flaunt it. Or, like Bernie Sanders, find a set of principles and keep them. Sanders, on the stump, was unequivocally himself.

The liberal left's obsession with Trump's strongman impulses masked, for the most part, the actual policy implications of his victory. The liberals did not talk about his desire to strip regulations from the financial markets and let the crypto-volk run wild, perhaps setting up the nation for another speculative bubble or something far worse. They failed to remind voters that Trump did not care whether they drank clean water because he would, inevitably, gut the EPA anew. More importantly, though, they had no vision for what came next because anti-fascism, on its own, lacks any kind of affirmative argument for tomorrow. Americans believe in democracy enough that they are betting Trump won't smash it apart. They want easier lives: cheaper housing, cheaper food, and cheaper healthcare. Culture matters too, and the social justice left never understood that either. Cosmopolitan demands don't work outside of college campuses and corporate boardrooms. The NGOs were never serious enough about the practice of politics in the streets of an inherently heterodox nation.

For those intrigued by newness, the second half of the 2020s might prove a tad more invigorating than the first. Trump is a retread, but the Democrats cannot be. All of their icons are vanquished. Obama single-handedly resuscitated two major political careers, and his country suffered for it; there is some Shakespeare in that. Biden was a failed presidential candidate until Obama made him his running mate in 2008. It was Biden's obstinance that yielded the great Democratic disaster of 2024. Hillary Clinton was a failed presidential candidate whom Obama appointed as his secretary of state and then decided, for reasons never entirely clear, to anoint as his successor. He bypassed Biden, his own vice president, who back then displayed no signs of senility. Biden might have beaten Trump in 2016. Instead, Biden backed away, using the death of his son as an excuse for what actually happened: Obama whipping elite donors and endorsers behind Clinton. This experience stuck with Biden and likely convinced him, during his first term, he could not give ground again.

Consider that run: Clinton, Biden, Harris. Three politicians who were inextricably bound to predecessor regimes. Three politicians who were not terribly talented. Prior to their respective presidential contests (nor after in Harris's case), none had triumphed in swing states. None had won, with any consistency, competitive statewide elections. None, most importantly, resembled Obama, who had no great dynasty or institution behind him, no legacy to be shackled by. Obama, like some cautionary Greek myth, could not learn the lessons that his own career should have taught him. A meteor burns bright, and Obama was blinded by his own light. Only he knows why he foisted Clinton on America. Now, like the rest of us, he will be forced to drink in another Trump term. The fading reality TV star he once mocked at that

Washington dinner will be, barring a health crisis, a two-term American president. Whereas Obama, eight years on, has plainly left little to the Democratic Party, Trump has thoroughly demolished and rebuilt the Republicans in his image. He is as consequential as Reagan and Nixon, and he might loom in American life just as long. The Trump era began when he descended the golden escalator in the middle of 2015, and it won't end until 2028 (potentially even later, if he follows through on his recent threats to seek a third term). The next Republican to run for president will not be able to do it without Trump's firm endorsement. His is a cult that is now far too large to be called one.

Now, for the Democrats, it is all wide open. There will be no one anointed in 2028. Instead, there will be a long, bloody fight for the nomination, and that is democracy. The liberal-left resistance, meanwhile, will have to stagger into a future they failed, over and over again, to head off. No movement, perhaps, has accomplished less. No movement has done so little to reach what was supposed to be an existential goal. Trump, eight years into the resistance, is at his apogee. The editorial boards and NGO bosses and magazine writers and braying congressmen and MSNBC panelists must contend with this bare, inarguable fact. The electoral map ran bloodred. How? Why? It was the racism of an Arab majority city voting for Trump, the white supremacy of the Bronx, New York's poorest borough, deciding Trump needed more of its votes than ever before. Pundits prattle about misinformation, as if all the voters were toddlers who needed to be bolted down and told why Brat Summer was so vital for the future of the republic. The liberal left reaps what it sows. It was not merely Trump that was chosen. It was the *not*-Democrat, the option that wasn't in power. A vote is a middle finger aimed at the sky. In the heat of all this, the liberal left will have to recalibrate or dissolve. Radical chic is fading. The Hitler analogies are played out. So are the speech wars. They will have to, somehow, consider material conditions. This is never easy if you've never lived anything close to a precarious life. Harder, still, if you've allowed condescension and indignation to become the pillars of a worldview. The smug never inherit the Earth. If only the Bible noted this, or someone took it to cable television in time. Much grief could have been averted.

On the morning of the presidential election, Alexandria Ocasio-Cortez released a memo. The star congresswoman, seeking re-election herself, wanted the media to know how much she had done for Kamala Harris and the rest of the Democratic Party. Her campaign wrote:

> Since August's Democratic National Convention in Chicago, Rep. Ocasio-Cortez has held more than 30 events in Wisconsin, Michigan, Pennsylvania, Texas, Nevada, and Puerto Rico to campaign for Vice President Harris, Democrats, and progressive candidates up and down the ticket . . . Over 7,500 people joined her at

these events across the country. Her campaign also supported getting thousands of volunteers to critical swing districts in Pennsylvania in the days before the election. Rep. Ocasio-Cortez on Monday closed out her national get out the vote effort with Vice President Harris at a Puerto Rican bakery in Reading, Pennsylvania.

"Videos on social media featuring Rep. Ocasio-Cortez consistently perform well," the campaign boasted, "and effectively move voters to support Democrats." There were statistics to make the case. A Twitch livestream with Tim Walz racked up 227,000 views. A response to Tony Hinchcliffe's "floating island of garbage" remark got 10.9 million impressions and 153,000 likes on Twitter/X. Her response to Trump's McDonald's outing earned 3.7 million plays and 235,000 likes on Instagram, 1.1 million views and 142,000 likes on TikTok, 1.7 million impressions and 23,000 likes on Twitter/X, and 450,000 views on YouTube.

The evolution of AOC has always intrigued me because she is the only famous politician I knew pre-fame. In 2017, I was the first journalist to interview her about her congressional campaign, and when I later ran for office myself, we chatted occasionally as fellow progressives trying to take on the Democratic establishment. We were both born in October 1989 and share generational commonalities: tough memories of 9/11, the financial crisis, and graduating into the kind of precarity that makes today's inflation seem rather tame.

I explain to the younger generations that everything was much cheaper in 2011 but there were hardly any decent jobs to be had and none of them seemed to pay a lot. I understood her career trajectory very well. And as someone who had written critically about the Queens Democratic Party, I was gratified that someone, at last, was challenging their boss, Joe Crowley.

In this election, Ocasio-Cortez was a proud foot solider of the Kamala Harris campaign. She stumped across America for the vice president, called Jill Stein's Green Party campaign "predatory"—best, for the Democrats, to have a young leftist do this—and delivered a rousing speech at the Democratic National Convention, where she praised Harris for "working tirelessly to achieve a ceasefire in Gaza." For many mainstream Democrats, 2024 was when the left-wing rebel grew up and joined the club. Suddenly, the MSNBC set didn't mind her at all. Whereas Bernie Sanders never seemed particularly enthusiastic about Harris, sensing perhaps she was eager to abandon Joe Biden's economic populism, AOC was all-in. If she were ten or twenty years older, there would have been chatter about a bid for a cabinet post in a Harris administration.

Until the night of November 5, these moves seemed canny, if ultimately cynical. How could Ocasio-Cortez, who once promised a political revolution herself, be so enthusiastic about a milquetoast product of the California Democratic establishment, a politician who, while racing to the center, was boasting about America's "lethal" military and her own prized handgun? Harris, on foreign policy, was an enigma, but no one could say with a straight face she was working "tirelessly" for a ceasefire as tens of thousands of Gazan bodies piled up. It wasn't as if Jake Sullivan or Lloyd Austin needed to seek advice from a former one-term senator from California. Throughout her career, Harris had been nurtured by power elite, and her presidential campaign was backed by many billionaires, including Barry Diller and Mark Cuban. Each were open about their desire for Harris to dump Lina Khan, Biden's Federal Trade Commission chair and the architect of his antitrust policy; their hope, plainly, was to elect a Democrat who was friendlier to corporate America and Silicon Valley. Harris had even made overtures to the cryptocurrency industry, indicating that their great enemy at the SEC, Gary Gensler, was living on borrowed time. *This* was AOC's candidate? But the democratic socialist is ambitious. She wants to be with a winner. Team players get further in DC, anyway.

The election did not go Ocasio-Cortez's way. This can be said of any Democrat. What's rough is that her campaigning came to so little. She outran Harris in her own district, but her Spanish-speaking constituents swerved hard toward Trump. After the "island of garbage" controversy, AOC all but promised an enormous wave of Puerto Rican voters would rise up against Trump. Instead, the nation's most prominent Puerto Rican politician looked on as heavily Puerto Rican neighborhoods in Pennsylvania and New York City gave more of their vote to Trump than they did in 2020. The youngest millennials and zoomers did not necessarily follow the lead of the politician who was supposed to be their generation's lodestar. In a sign of a burgeoning counterculture that the liberal left would love to discipline out of existence, more and more of them chose the incendiary Trump.

Ocasio-Cortez has spoken about an "inside-outside" political strategy which pairs outside organizing and agitation with the painstaking work of legislating within institutions. She's been a diligent congresswoman, no doubt, and the progressive left in America has been better off for her advocacy. What she may soon come to understand, however, is that one cannot be inside *and* outside in perpetuity. This election demonstrated that she has mostly made her choice. She wants to be an insider. She might want to chair the Congressional Progressive Caucus one day or run for the Senate in New York. A presidential bid feels inevitable. She might be potent in a Democratic primary for president, although her grip on the electorate—that progressive and Latino coalition—suddenly seems tenuous. If she's another center-left lawmaker, how will she distinguish herself in a crowded presidential field? She's got years to ponder that.

What AOC has plainly decided not to do is be a genuine leader of the American left. Sanders does not have a successor. Were he a decade younger, he would probably be contemplating a third presidential bid. This may speak more to a paucity of current options on the left than to any greater vanity on Sanders's part. Sanders is not a terribly introspective politician and, even in his eighties, he has seemed to give little thought to what will happen to his movement after he's gone. He's an important figure in American history, but he's not the organizer or party boss progressives and socialists need to increase their power in the future. He has, for good reason, returned to the news cycle because a growing number of Democrats are waking to the reality that his political instincts in 2016 were largely correct: you win on economics, and you can't lurch too far to the left on culture. The Hillary Clinton wing of the party deemed Sanders a racist ("If we broke up the big banks tomorrow . . . would that end racism? Would that end sexism?") and soundly rejected his contention, even after the fall of *Roe v. Wade*, that campaigning on abortion rights wouldn't be enough to keep winning. He was chastened in 2022, but it became obvious, as the presidential election neared, that voters were supportive of referendums legalizing abortion but were not otherwise reflexively choosing Harris. They needed something else to vote for—promises to bring down the cost of groceries, the cost of rent, and the interest rates. Some also wanted a tighter border.

Sanders fits much more neatly into this matrix than Ocasio-Cortez. He has called the concept of open borders a "Koch brothers" proposal. He never wanted to defund the police. And he has embraced alternative, dissident media. When running for president in 2020, he appeared on Joe Rogan's podcast. Rogan was smitten enough that he endorsed Sanders. The fresh calls for a "Democratic" Rogan to counteract the Trumpian right miss a much more brutal truth: these voters were there for the taking, if only Democrats bothered to listen to them. Ocasio-Cortez, for all her youth and savvy, couldn't grasp the future as well as a man born during World War II. After the Sanders campaign promoted his appearance on Rogan, Ocasio-Cortez refused to aggressively stump for him in the early voting states. During one campaign speech in Iowa, she even declined to mention Sanders's name. This was the height of the social justice era, and Ocasio-Cortez was at its vanguard. Progressives, preaching a big tent, were rhetorically closing it in the name of protecting the marginalized. Rogan did not belong, and those who enabled Rogan did not belong. A year later, in the wake of the George Floyd protests, Ross Douthat of the *Times* posited that Sanders had lost the future. "Rather than Medicare for All and taxing plutocrats, the rallying cry is racial justice and defunding the police," he wrote. "Instead of finding its nemeses in corporate suites, the intersectional revolution finds them on antique pedestals and atop the cultural establishment."

This had been true. Now, a new era blooms, and the intersectional left—the so-called woke—is falling out of vogue. Politics and culture are untethering again.

Trump's return will not reverse a trend that had been accelerating for the last three years. Ocasio-Cortez, for all her association with democratic socialism, was an identity-first liberal at heart, someone who was fully fluent in the language of the professional class. Sanders, who grew up poorer than she did and never abandoned the Marxist flavorings of his youth, could never operate in that mode. He believed, fully, in the dream of a multiracial working-class coalition. He knew, to get there, he would have to knit together disparate clusters of human beings—those, in fact, who held views that might be considered impolitic or even ugly. There was no shunning Rogan if that was your grand goal: the working class listened to him, and so Sanders would go there. This was why he showed up on Fox News, too.

Sanders is not always a nimble thinker. While calling himself a socialist—and limiting his appeal, ultimately, among the broader electorate—he has done little to bolster the only functioning socialist organization in the United States. Our Revolution, which was supposed to be the vehicle for Sanders's politics, has amounted to little. What Sanders has bequeathed to Democrats is a comprehension, finally, of the need for a class-based politics, one that takes material need seriously. If Sanders was a college graduate, he rarely spoke like one, and he understood why politics had to be made tangible. And for the sake of the left itself, he grasped that it was vital to hold yourself *beyond* the Democratic establishment. For some socialists, ironically, Sanders was always viewed as too accommodating, endorsing both Clinton and Biden and campaigning for them. He certainly championed the Biden administration. Now, upon Harris's loss, he is blasting away at the Democratic establishment anew.

Ocasio-Cortez is not. She is not at the forefront of this new reckoning over what a defeated party needs to do. She has a bright a future in Washington if she remains in Congress; she can accumulate seniority, chair committees when the Democrats eventually win the House, and perhaps wait out Chuck Schumer's retirement. What she will not be is the next leader of the American left. Perhaps she doesn't want this any longer and is more comfortable playing surrogate for whomever party elites anoint. She didn't *have to* campaign harder for Harris than she ever did for Sanders. She obviously felt motivated. A more difficult question for her might be, as the decade wears on, where her political base truly resides. If Latinos are too culturally conservative for her and young leftists drift away, who does she have? Will she, one day, see the utility of Joe Rogan or Lex Fridman or Theo Von and go where the young now congregate? Will she break from her professional class cloister? If not, she'll only matter so much.

The professional class can never fully comprehend Donald Trump; most of the professional class did not grow up in the boroughs surrounding Manhattan. This does not mean there's any great folk wisdom to be had on Parsons Boulevard or the Grand Concourse or Bay Ridge Parkway. It only means that a Weltanschauung can be forged by where one lives, and if Trump and I don't have very much in common, we do share this: we are products of outer-borough life. "One of the longest journeys in the world is the journey from Brooklyn to Manhattan—or at least from certain neighborhoods in Brooklyn to certain parts of Manhattan," the Brownsville-reared Norman Podhoretz wrote more than a half century ago. If the divide between the boroughs has narrowed since then, with gentrification metastasizing, this is still not wrong. To certain residents of Brooklyn, Queens, the Bronx, and Staten Island, Manhattan will always be the City: gleaming, remote, the locus of great envy and resentment, the terminus of a long, creaking subway ride.

Or allow me a caveat—the non-Manhattan neighborhoods in closest proximity to Manhattan do not share the outer-borough mindset any longer. The professional class is too ensconced there. Once, neighborhoods like Park Slope and Carroll Gardens, when they were brawling Irish strongholds, *did*. Dumbo, beneath the Manhattan Bridge, was an industrial outpost. Williamsburg and Greenpoint were for working stiffs, the Polish and the Puerto Ricans. These days, they belong to the mid-level financiers, nonprofit executives, and upwardly mobile youth who make up the spine of the Democratic Party. Among the professional class who live in the coveted outer-borough neighborhoods—those that have properly gentrified—there is a term used to discuss and dismiss the rest, one I've come to resent: *deep*. Are you in *deep* Brooklyn or *deep* Queens? *Depth* is a measure of how far you are from Manhattan as well as the cultural exports of the neighborhoods considered to lie in proper commuting distance. It is time measured on the subway, as well as a greater psychological chasm that will not be crossed. Life isn't quite *happening*, they imply, in deep Brooklyn or deep Queens. Not like in Bushwick or Astoria.

Trump grew up in Jamaica Estates, an affluent enclave bordering working-class Jamaica, Queens. The residents there do not cross Hillside Avenue to rove among the Black sections of Jamaica unless they must. Trump's father, Fred, was a wealthy real estate developer who built a great deal of housing in Brooklyn and Queens for largely white families who belonged to the working and middle classes. Fred's projects were unfashionable but lucrative, dun-colored and dependable. There was no glitz, only power; Fred was a patron of the local Democratic machines, and there wasn't a governor or mayor who wouldn't take his phone calls. Fred did not resent being an outer-borough builder. He had grown rich that way. His brash, bilious son, however, did not want to remain in Queens, or at the family office on Avenue Z in Sheepshead Bay. He wanted *Manhattan*.

If there is a single way, still, to understand Donald Trump, the forty-fifth and forty-seventh president of the

United States, it's to recall the boy gazing out onto the vast, glassy plain of the City and wishing, more than anything else in this life, to belong to that—to be *of it*, fully, and perhaps one day be its king. What Trump knows is that he can dominate America but not Manhattan. The Manhattan elites will not take him seriously. The builders there know who built what, who owns what, who has credit and who does not. They know he is a comic book's idea of a rich person, a fantasy he willed into being but is still an illusion. Trump is now in Florida because they will have him there. West Palm Beach receives garish Donald J. as one of their own. The New York rich, meanwhile, are ruthlessly discreet, as are most of the American families, often WASP, who found their fortunes more than a century ago and tend to their titanic inheritances in cool, comforting shadow. They armor themselves on Park or Fifth or on Central Park West, and they'd rather waft through charity dinners than run for office themselves. Michael Bloomberg was the exception, not the rule. The ruling class is not interested in downgrading to Gracie Mansion or the White House. A rube could take Trump Tower seriously, but not a billionaire, and Trump only found the legitimacy he craved through elected office. Fred asked for favors. Donald wanted to be the man granting them.

The outer-borough drive to power can be harnessed for good or ill alike. It's not an accident that many of the greatest artists of the last century came from Brooklyn, Queens, and the Bronx, and that exceedingly ambitious people have long battled toward Manhattan, lured onward by Big City glory. If wielded correctly, this outer-borough resentment is manna. *I'll show them* produces your best work, vaults you into stations once unimaginable. It's not so different from the Midwestern boys and girls who want to make it big in the East—except, perhaps, resentment burns brighter in those who are most near the City's roar. Anguish, too. Few works of art capture this better than *Saturday Night Fever*. Filmed in the Brooklyn neighborhood of Bay Ridge, where I grew up, the John Travolta flick is recalled as a gauzy paean to disco. Those who've watched it closely know the 1977 film, one of the best of its era, is an unsparing view of white, working-class malaise in a swath of the borough that is, psychically, much further than one subway ride. Travolta's Tony Manero begins to long for escape, but can't quite break free from his old pals, who have no ambitions beyond Saturday night. His love interest, Stephanie, hungers to get through the tunnel and cement herself in the City; she chides Tony for not seeming to want more out of his life except dancing and sex. Between the iconic dance scenes, there's a gang rape and a death on the Verrazzano-Narrows Bridge. Tony needs to decide whether he can break away.

The Bay Ridge of my childhood was much more bucolic than that; it was the 1990s, not the 1970s, and I took a healthier view of Manhattan because both my mother and father worked there. It was a very Republican neighborhood then. As a Jew, I was in a distinct minority, which surprises those who imagine there are as many New York Jews sprinkled around the five boroughs as fire hydrants. It was heavily Irish and Italian and Catholic, as well as Greek Orthodox. The Asian and Arab populations were growing. One of the more amusing turns of the last few years has been the emergence of the "rad-trad" aesthetic, the bid of certain self-declared dissidents to ostentatiously convert to Catholicism to irritate secular liberals. Anyone who grew up in outer-borough New York would understand Catholicism to be the least subversive religion (or pose) imaginable. Churches seem to spring up on every other Bay Ridge block. As a teen, I played for baseball teams sponsored by St. Patrick's, St. Bernadette's, and St. Francis Xavier. I took the antisemitic taunts from Catholic boys who were speaking more from ignorance than malice. I still enjoyed Christmastime, because the lights on the houses, as gaudy as they could be, shone lovingly in the dark.

There was fighting. Kids in certain neighborhoods, of certain eras, had to shove or punch eventually. I was not a large child, nor especially tough. I never thought of myself as a fighter. And yet, surveying my memory, I realize I was in at least four physical fights, including a tussle in the dugout with a teammate when I was sixteen. He had put a used condom in my glove and I, in retaliation, knocked his hat off and stomped on it. He punched me, I swung back, and the coach booted us both from the field. Tempers seemed to always run hot. Parochial, sure, but there was an honor culture one had to abide by. Talk shit, get hit. Two bits of Trump lore I understood intuitively, from growing up in southern Brooklyn: locker-room talk and hitting someone back as hard—or harder—than they hit you.

The outer boroughs like Trump as much as any American hinterland. Each cycle, he grows his vote there. It's not just the whites anymore, the elderly Tony Maneros and their swaggering children affixing MAGA flags to their attached homes. The whitelash thesis lies as dead as Kamala Harris's political career. The Chinese of Bensonhurst have grown into staunch Republicans. The Latinos of Corona seem headed there. Don't even ask about the Russian and Orthodox Jews who once, from time to time, split their tickets for local Democrats and barely do now. Manhattan is now trending bluest, more than the Bronx, still the poorest of the five boroughs. What Trump was selling, many of the working class were buying—or, simply, they found the Democrats, at home and abroad in Washington, had nothing much to offer them anymore. In Fred Trump's day, the Democratic organizations were *organizations*. They whipped voters block to block, inserted themselves into neighborhood struggles, and ensured their local clubs were packed with volunteers. They dispensed patronage, but it wasn't as if every Democratic voter was getting a job with the city. They wanted to belong to a kind of civic life, and the machines had that to give. Now the organizations carry on as phantoms, as after-images of a different age. The machines hardly run at all.

In the Democratic Party, Trump sees Manhattan. His followers see Manhattan, too. They exult because they have won, but they lack all patrician grace, or the self-assuredness a technocratic, managerial party might bring to bear in victory. They are ruddy and angry and anxious. They know, when their thoughts go quiet and the TV's turned down low, this is *it*—this is the zenith. Second-term presidents get unpopular. Majorities slip away. Opponents wise up. An outer borough will not just become an inner borough. Trump's policies are insider policies (tax cuts for the rich, right-wing judges for the courts), but he will never govern like an insider, like someone who belongs in the seat of power. He seems to not care, but I will hazard that he just might—that he longs, in his singular demented way, to be another Lincoln or Roosevelt, a man infused with enough gravity to endure through the centuries. When Stephanie is telling Tony he has to get serious about his life and get out of the neighborhood, there's a poignancy to her harangues; she sounds so much like she's from Bay Ridge, going on about what's ref*eye*ned and which direc*tuh* she likes and what the women in the *awe*ffice drink. If Tony is a troglodyte to her, Manhattan audiences sneer at them both. Even when you cross the bridge, the neighborhood comes with you. It's in your voice and lodged in your heart.

8

The Changing Resistance

On the social media site formerly known as Twitter, the famed *Times* journalist Nikole Hannah-Jones claimed Donald Trump's victory was a function of "anti-Blackness" and misogyny. David Corn, the prominent *Mother Jones* reporter, fumed about Russia interfering with another presidential election. A random person in my feed screamed about light-skinned Latino men dooming the country. One woman said all women should stop dating and having sex with men.

It was easy to think, consuming these dispatches in the wake of Trump's resurgence and the utter destruction of Kamala Harris's presidential campaign, that the manias of 2016 and 2017 were repeating themselves. For months, I've wondered whether a potential Trump triumph could trigger the rise of a new so-called Resistance or a mass revival of the social justice left—or *woke*, although I find that term a bit wearying and imprecise. Now that Trump has won a far larger victory than he did eight years ago, would we be returning to a version of those times, when Trump's madness drove his opponents all the madder and men like Robert Mueller were sanctified?

The answer, I found in the late autumn of 2024, was an emphatic *no*. The above social media posts were liked enough, but they were the equivalent of hearty shouts at a windswept sea.

This is not to undersell the damage a Trump restoration has caused. Trump's courts and bureaucracy could further undercut abortion rights. He is guting environmental regulations. His corporate tax and Medicaid cuts will worsen income inequality. Other social safety net programs for the poor can be weakened. His Justice Department, in the case of Mahmoud Khalil and others, is blatantly violating the First Amendment. New money (Elon Musk and DOGE) and old money (the Kochs) are running roughshod over the federal government. Joe Biden's progressive economic legacy is in peril.

The lack of a new 2017-style resistance is not to be bemoaned; it speaks to the growing maturity of America and, I hope, the realization that such histrionics were ultimately unsuccessful. The anti-Trump movement lost. Haranguing the media for "normalizing" Trump and demanding that Democrats keep calling Trump a liar or fascist did nothing. Trump simply came back stronger. The old anti-Trump resistance, a cottage industry of aggrieved Republicans nostalgic for the Bush years and MSNBC liberals who wailed about the evil Orange Man and his subservience to Vladimir Putin, had no coherent message beyond Trump's inherent unsuitability for office and their belief that voters, over time, could be browbeaten into blindly supporting Democrats. The culmination of it all was Trump becoming the first Republican to win the popular vote in twenty years.

The initial Trump-era protests were largely unfocused and self-satisfied. They had limited structure and deficient leaders—if they possessed leaders at all. The Women's March crumbled away. Black Lives Matter devolved. Serious organizers sat at the helm of the civil rights and feminist movements of the 1960s and 1970s, and material change was won. The upsurges of the 2010s and 2020, when George Floyd was killed, amounted to spectacle and little else. Some laws did change on the criminal justice front, and progressive prosecutors were swept into office, but there was little thought given to the long term, to building durable organizations that would outlive the boom times. Movements cannot rise on froth alone.

This hyperpolitics, as the academic Anton Jäger has called it, lived online. Its manna was the pre–Elon Musk Twitter and Facebook when it wasn't suppressing news links. The digital realm allowed for fast organizing and faster disappearance. Posting felt like its own act of resistance. Tweet hard enough, the psychology went, and good things might happen. Trump, then, was Twitter's king, and the media hung on every demented dispatch. The resistance never ran out of outrage. It was a toxic cycle that pleased everyone. Trumpists could brag about owning the libs. Liberals could feel the catharsis of an ocean of retweets.

Little of it was tethered to material conditions. A few

leftists offered an alternative path but couldn't quite rise above the tide. Bernie Sanders, in 2016, had the correct instincts; he understood where the nation was headed and spoke to some of the same anguish and distrust in elites that would lead to Trump's presidency. Sanders ran on class struggle, denouncing free-trade agreements and the deindustrialization of the Midwest. He promised universal health care. He didn't dismiss identity concerns—he had marched in the civil rights movement, and his record on social justice was strong—but he believed it was economics that would unite the white, Hispanic, Black, and Asian working classes of America. The Hillary Clinton campaign dismissed him as a racist, and the Democratic establishment strained to suppress him as much as they could. Clinton won more votes, but Sanders upsetting her in Michigan was the warning shot that the smug former first lady chose to ignore. We know what happened next.

Among despondent Democrats today, there is much chatter about alternative media. Some think Musk's X fed so much disinformation into the electorate that all of these voters chose Trump. They claim that the *correct* information would have saved Harris, as if a campaign devoid of a message or genuine rationale for running just needed media coverage that was a bit more sycophantic and widespread. It is true that the collapse of regional newspapers has fed conspiracy theories and, in some form, enabled a charlatan like Trump. It is also true that in the largest media market in America, New

York City, Trump won the highest share of any Republican candidate since the 1980s. But if Democrats actually care about the alternative and the dissident, they had their chance and blew it.

There will be elections in 2026, and again in 2028. The dying embers of the resistance might wish otherwise, if only to be right about something for once. There is much, of course, to resist and combat in Trump's governance. He won full control of Congress. The policy that comes from that government could immiserate the working class. Resisting it all will require the kind of discipline and sobriety that the 2010s ideological warriors never learned.

Joe Biden exited the White House with as little fanfare as any president in modern memory. Forever sandwiched between Donald Trump presidencies and unwilling, in his eighties, to engage with conventional media for any length of time—there are few interviews, televised or in print, for Americans to grasp on to—he will recede, lost in various Trump- and Musk-fired news cycles. "It is hard," Peter Baker of the *New York Times* wrote, "to imagine that he seriously thought he could do the world's most stressful job for another four years."

This is now conventional wisdom, in the way opposition to the Iraq War, as the 2000s wore on and the Middle East further destabilized, became the new political consensus. Many pundits, journalists, and politicians who supported the war either recanted or pretended they were on the right side all along. Trump himself fell into the latter camp, blasting away at his war-supporting GOP rivals in the 2016 primary despite his own documented support for the invasion in 2003. If many politicians and media elites never had to pay much of a political price for getting history so wrong, they at least had to grapple, in some form, with their failure. Some, like Andrew Sullivan, were refreshingly candid about why they had trusted George W. Bush in the first place.

The conspiracy of silence around Biden's age-related decline does not rise to the level of the cognoscenti's embrace of the Iraq War—it did not lead to the deaths of thousands of American troops and many more Iraqi civilians—but it does, in its enforcement of a remarkably foolhardy groupthink, demand its own kind of reckoning. And it's not at all apparent such a reckoning will ever come. As trust in the media plummets and the Democratic Party itself limps into a murky future, once again locked out of power in Washington, probing questions must be asked of how, for years on end, so many influential people insisted Biden was capable of not only campaigning again but governing for another four years.

The *Wall Street Journal* extensively documented how Biden's inner circle limited contact with other administration officials, politicians, donors, and journalists, privately acknowledging the elderly Biden could not perform the duties of a president. At events, aides often repeated instructions to Biden, telling him where to enter or exit a stage. As early as his first year in the White

House, aides were canceling meetings when Biden seemed "off." "He has good days and bad days, and today was a bad day so we're going to address this tomorrow," a former aide recalled a national security official saying, according to the *Journal*. Meetings, the newspaper reported, were started later in the day because Biden seemed to struggle early in the morning. Most members of Congress, meanwhile, couldn't talk to Biden at all. Staff locked him away. The implication was that the president simply wasn't able to sustain complex, one-on-one interactions.

Will 2024 be remembered for the assassination attempt on Trump's life and the "fight fight fight" photo? Or for Biden dropping out of the race after the worst televised performance in the history of presidential debates? Both, perhaps, but it's the Biden chaos that might linger longer in history, since Americans have a habit of forgetting the would-be assassins—Thomas Crooks, in this case—who shoot at presidents and don't kill them. (Neither of the women who attempted to kill Gerald Ford are remembered, apart from Squeaky Fromme's association with Charles Manson, and John Hinckley only endures, vaguely, because he was deeply obsessed with Jodie Foster.)

Baker's report in the *Times* on Biden's diminishment reflects the retroactive consensus: *Of course* Biden could never really run again or theoretically govern the nation until he was eighty-six. Except virtually every Democrat and left-leaning pundit insisted otherwise until the June debate between Biden and Trump, and much of the media was glad to portray age-related concerns as a right-wing disinformation operation. The *Times*, in the days before the debate, warned of a "distorted, online version of himself, a product of often misleading videos that play into and reinforce voters' longstanding concerns about his age and abilities." Dana Milbank of the *Washington Post* said he found the "fretting over Biden's age tedious" and blamed it on "disinformation from the right portraying him as drooling and senile." Margaret Sullivan, the veteran journalist and media critic, dismissed chatter about Biden's cognition and performance as ageism. Joe Scarborough declared, infamously, that "this version of Biden, intellectually, analytically, is the best Biden ever."

Democrats themselves were no less insistent on Biden's fitness. As late as July, Gavin Newsom, the governor of California, was calling Biden "extraordinarily competent." "You need to let Joe Biden be Joe Biden," Michigan representative Debbie Dingell insisted earlier that year. When Dean Phillips, a representative from Minnesota, launched a long-shot primary campaign against Biden, citing the president's age as a central motivator for running, he endured resentment and rage from the Democratic establishment. "I don't understand what his goals are. I just don't understand," said Colorado senator John Hickenlooper. Pramila Jayapal, the chair of the Congressional Progressive Caucus, was no less dismissive. "I'm sorry, I have no idea what he's running on that's different from what President Biden is running on."

A retrospective narrative of the Biden years is that it took too long for the truth to come out, but that Democrats shouldn't be blamed for not understanding Biden's deficiencies until the summer of 2024. After waving away criticisms of Biden's age-related stumbles, Matthew Yglesias wrote that "zero information has leaked into the public domain suggesting that Biden is behind the scenes incapable of doing the job." Once Biden struggled to speak coherently on television with Trump, Yglesias noted, while calling for Biden to step aside, that "it was correct to withhold judgment until we saw the debate." Yet this plainly was *not* correct. Yglesias shouldn't be singled out here, since he was one of many prominent Democrats who believed such a falsehood, but he is emblematic of a blinkered worldview that directly led to the return of President Trump.

I wrote, in September 2022, that Biden shouldn't seek another term. I was not a White House reporter, an elected official, or a special insider with great insights into the Biden administration. I simply used my own eyes and ears. Biden, by then, was already mangling basic statistics in public remarks and calling Kamala Harris the "president." Soon after, he would claim his son, Beau, died in Iraq and not of brain cancer. He would ask whether a congresswoman who had recently died was at one of his White House events. It was obvious, if you consumed any amount of news and weren't willfully blinding yourself, that something was deeply amiss. (Baker himself, days before the 2022 midterms, noted these Biden stumbles—but the *Times* did not produce much in-depth reporting on his decline in the subsequent year and a half.)

What does it say about the Democratic Party and the media broadly that Biden's presidency was essentially ended by the simple act of showing up on television to debate his opponent? As cable TV ratings crater and traditional media struggles to maintain the trust it has left, this question should haunt the many political elites who giddily lied to themselves and others for three and a half years. What *is* worse, ignorance or outright deception? Democrats and their allies in the media engaged in both. Now Trump reigns again. Whatever happens over the next four years, the Democratic Party certainly earned it.

If the first election of Donald Trump was a boon to the progressive wing of the Democratic Party, the second might have granted new life to cultural moderates. Trump's popular vote victory—his only, and one of the most dispiriting events for the American left in the twenty-first century—put to rest several long-standing arguments about the national electorate. It was far easier to blame racism for Trump's shock win in 2016 because Barack Obama had stumped aggressively for Hillary Clinton, who still beat Trump by two percentage points. Eight years later, Trump has made tremendous gains with Latino, Asian, and even some Black voters, and his 2024 coalition was more multiracial than any liberal pundit would have predicted just a few years ago.

In turn, many of the de rigueur causes of the 2010s have fallen out of vogue. Black Live Matter is moribund, and there are no calls to abolish ICE despite Trump promising mass deportations. The Women's March didn't materialize to oppose Trump's inauguration. Climate activism, which burned so hot in the late 2010s and early 2020s, is at a low ebb, and despite David Hogg's rise to vice-chair of the Democratic National Committee, there is nothing approximating the mass marches over gun control that took place in 2018 and 2019. Trump's repeated attacks on so-called DEI initiatives and "woke" have triggered only limited backlash from Democrats, who seem increasingly willing to move on from culture war.

The latest evidence of a possible moderate resurgence was a gathering hosted by Third Way, the centrist Democratic think tank, in February 2025. Unlike the DNC, which has not performed any autopsy of 2024, Third Way produced five pages of takeaways that it believes explain Democratic failure and how to plot a path back to power. They blame a failure to prioritize economic concerns, an overemphasis on identity politics, allowing the "far-left" to define the party, and an attachment to unpopular institutions like academia, the media, and government bureaucracy for Trump's ascendance. Among Third Way's proposals is a ban on "far-left candidate questionnaires" and a movement "away from the dominance of small-dollar donors whose preferences may not align with the broader electorate." They argued, too, for Democrats to embrace "patriotism, community, and traditional American imagery" and to "get out of elite circles and into real communities" like tailgates, gun shows, local restaurants, and churches. It was time, they proclaimed, to celebrate "moderation, individualism, and masculinity."

Given the slow bleed of working-class voters from the Democratic Party, especially men, much of this is sound reasoning—if easy to mock on social media. Ruben Gallego, the new Democratic senator from Arizona, told the *New York Times* that the left needs to understand that "every Latino man wants a big-ass truck." Democrats are afraid, Gallego said, of "saying, like, 'Hey, let's help you get a job so you can become rich.' " The GOP, for many voters, has become the aspirational, freedom-loving party, while Democrats embody the nattering, faculty-lounge caricature, too affluent and alien. There is an *image* problem that Democrats will need to fix. Pumping out new policy platforms isn't enough.

But the battle back to power—and the hope for Democrats, really, of erecting any sort of sustainable and durable majority—will be far more complicated than simply pivoting to the center. Behind Third Way's argument that small donors represent an energized minority that could force certain Democrats to take unpopular positions is the implication that *large* donors are a safer bet—as if millionaires and billionaires weren't capable of corroding the priorities of politicians and dragging them away from where the median voter might be. If it's understandable Third Way doesn't want Democrats to be openly "anti-capitalist" (capitalism itself polls well, after all), the plea for Democrats "to stop demonizing wealth and corporations broadly" is odder.

What evidence is there that corporate skepticism has damaged either party? Were it up to Third Way, Trump would never have turned against NAFTA and Obama would have tried to triangulate John McCain on economics, running to the right as the financial sector collapsed in 2008. Bernie Sanders's enduring popularity, including his recent, packed-out rallies against oligarchy, should be impossible. Sanders, the self-identified socialist from Vermont, has always confounded Third Way, never more so than during his 2016 presidential campaign, when he won more than 40 percent of the primary vote.

Sanders never became president, and several of his most prominent protégés, among them Alexandria Ocasio-Cortez, embody some of the 2010s and early '20s excesses that cost Democrats votes, such as calls to defund the police and comparisons of migrant detention facilities to "concentration camps." But Sanders himself, even at the height of the George Floyd protests, was against pulling funding from police departments, instead enraging progressives by reiterating his belief that officers should be paid more money. On immigration, Sanders is far more humane than any Republican but has decried an open border, likening it to a scheme for the wealthy to procure cheap labor. A supporter of gun control, Sanders was nevertheless more moderate than many cultural liberals because he had risen to power in a rural state where Republicans once held great sway.

A more culturally right-wing version of Sanders almost nabbed a Senate seat in deep-red Nebraska last year, and it's peculiar that many Democrats, including Third Way, still don't want to talk about it. Dan Osborn came within seven points of defeating Deb Fischer, an incumbent Republican, in a state Trump would carry by more than twenty points. Osborn, a mechanic and labor leader, had led a strike at Kellogg's Omaha plant in 2021; on economic issues, he represented everything that Third Way, which is Clintonian centrist at its core, resents. He supported raising the national minimum wage, bolstering railway safety, strengthening Social Security, and making it easier for workers to organize into labor unions. On culture, he did pivot right: He backed Trump's border wall and gun rights. He notably campaigned as an independent, not a Democrat, and targeted the very small donors Third Way wants Democrats to shun. Osborn did not commit to caucusing with the Democrats if he won, but at minimum, he would not have been an automatic vote for Trump in the Senate.

Most Democrats now agree that they have a *Senate* problem: The 2024 election cycle was not as devastating for Democrats as initially feared, with slim victories in Nevada, Michigan, and Wisconsin, but even this slight overperformance has resulted in a comfortable 53-47 GOP majority. To escape the minority and eventually find a way to fifty-two or fifty-three seats, Democrats will have to compete, as Third Way and many others argue, for working class and non–college-educated voters, especially in rural areas. This will mean, in addition to fixing the Democratic brand, fielding more candidates like Osborn who can make Trump states competitive again. It will not mean abandoning small donors or the economic populism that thrills them. It will mean being a tribune for the working class.